The Social Media Journali Handbook

D0705979

The Social Media Journalist Handbook teaches readers how to be a real-world social media journalist, tracing the evolution of the field to its current-day practice. This book establishes social media journalism as the latest and one of the most effective ways to practice journalism in the 21st century. It features insights from top recruiters, editors, and senior producers working in the field, as well as exercises that aid readers in developing the practical skills necessary to work successfully with social media. Readers will come away from the book with the knowledge to build strong social media strategies across different budgets, employing evergreen principles that work for different, ever-changing platforms. They'll learn how to reach and engage with the maximum number of people, as well as find sources, raise one's profile, conduct research, and produce stories. This book also features additional material online for instructors.

Yumi Wilson is an Associate Professor of Journalism at San Francisco State University where she has taught since 2004. She also works as a social media consultant and trainer.

The Social Media Journalist Handbook

Yumi Wilson

Routledge
Taylor & Francis Group

NEW YORK AND LONDON

First edition published 2019
by Routledge
52 Vanderbilt Avenue, New York, NY 10017

and by Routledge
2 Park Square, Milton Park, Abingdon, Oxon, OX14 4RN

Routledge is an imprint of the Taylor & Francis Group, an informa business

© 2019 Taylor & Francis

The right of Yumi Wilson to be identified as author of this work
has been asserted by her in accordance with sections 77 and 78 of
the Copyright, Designs and Patents Act 1988.

All rights reserved. No part of this book may be reprinted or
reproduced or utilised in any form or by any electronic, mechanical,
or other means, now known or hereafter invented, including
photocopying and recording, or in any information storage or
retrieval system, without permission in writing from the publishers.

Trademark notice: Product or corporate names may be trademarks
or registered trademarks, and are used only for identification and
explanation without intent to infringe.

Library of Congress Cataloging-in-Publication Data
A catalog record has been requested for this book

ISBN: 9781138545694 (hbk)
ISBN: 9781138545700 (pbk)
ISBN: 9781351002622 (ebk)

Typeset in Bembo
by Swales & Willis Ltd, Exeter, Devon, UK

Visit the eResource: www.routledge.com/9781138545700

Contents

Acknowledgments

I'd like to thank Ross Wagenhofer, who helped me turn this dream of mine into reality with Routledge. Thanks to students at San Francisco State University for providing insight and encouragement along the road. Huge thanks to Andrea Crowley-Hughes for copyediting the book and creating the figures table and glossary. I'd also like to thank Gina Baleria of San Francisco State University and Grace Provenzano of Iowa State University for taking part in countless workshops and panels on social media in journalism. And a big thanks to my partner, Art Hartinger, for sticking next to me through countless hours of sleepless nights while writing this book.

List of Illustrations

Introduction

Once upon a time, big-name news outlets such as *The New York Times* and *60 Minutes* were the arbiters of news for the American people. Owners, publishers, editors, news directors, and producers were considered the gate-keepers of news vital to public discourse, determining which stories to high-light, how and when to present them, and who to feature in those stories. In 1897, Adolph S. Ochs, then the owner of *The New York Times*, created the "All the News That's Fit to Print" slogan in the hope of becoming the most trusted and reliable source of news for the American public.[1]

Fast forward to the 21st century.

While *The New York Times* remains a well-respected news provider to this day, trust in the media is at one of its lowest points in history[2] and it remains deeply divided along partisan lines.[3]

Americans "increasingly perceive the media as biased and struggle to identify objective news sources," according to the authors of the 2017 Gallup/Knight Foundation Survey on Trust, Media and Democracy. "They believe the media continue to have a critical role in our democracy but are not very positive about how the media are fulfilling that role."[4]

Additionally, thousands of bloggers and alternative media outlets around the world are capturing and sharing their own version of news, some focusing more on entertaining people than informing them. On their own, these new town criers lack the brand recognition of *The New York Times* or *60 Minutes*. However, thanks to sweeping advances in technology and the popularity of social media, almost anyone with the right equipment and resources has the potential to reach a mass audience.

"The rise of social media over the last ten years has seen a significant influence on the way in which news is reported and digested by all par-ties within journalism, with traditional journalists taking on a developed role utilizing social media as both a way to deliver and to promote their work," wrote Cheney Thomas in his master's thesis for the University of Gothenburg in Sweden.[5]

Perhaps even more important is a dramatic change in consumer hab-its. Ask any college student struggling to pay for books, rent, and food whether they subscribe to a newspaper or pay for cable TV – the answer will probably be no. Ask the same student whether they heard about the 4.5 earthquake or the protest on campus – the answer will probably be yes. That's because students are learning about the news through other channels of communication.

"I learned about the Florida high school shooting through iPhone's News mobile application," said a student at San Francisco State University. "I obtained more information regarding the shooting through a Google search, which prompted various articles and updates regarding the tragedy. These updates were available through multiple journalists on social media platforms such as Twitter and Facebook, which in turn has become a major source of information for many digital consumers."

This San Fransisco State student is not alone. The number of young people (aged 18 to 29) getting news from TV is down to 23 percent, according to the Pew Research Center.[6] "Even older Americans are relying less on television for news.[7] Just 50 percent of U.S. adults now get news regularly from television, down from 57 percent a year prior in early 2016," the Pew Research Center reported in September 2018.

The reason? Sweeping advances in technology and the Internet have made it easy and affordable to do almost everything by phone. Consumers can access news when and how they want through mobile apps, and journalists can report, produce, disseminate, and even promote the news through mobile media.

Thus, the relationship between the traditional news media and the audience has irrevocably changed.[8] Even as the Edelman Trust Barometer shows that trust in traditional news media is rebounding,[9] big media companies no longer hold a monopoly on news.

Citizen journalists, bloggers, advocates, and almost everyone have the ability to share news and information, not just with their friends or family, but with the world. And the audience is listening,[10] often choosing personalities or news sites that align with their values.

Seeking to adapt to the changes and appeal to this new audience, many traditional news companies are hiring journalists equally adept at reporting writing, editing, and producing the news as they are at creating and curating powerful and engaging content for both digital and social media.

Indeed, the duties of today's journalist have changed dramatically. A brief scan of the 2,600 attendees for the 2018 Online News Association (ONA) conference in Austin, Texas revealed that journalists at the *Seattle Times*, *Tribune-Review*, *WFAA*, *Chicago Sun-Times*, *NBCUniversal*, and hundreds of other news outlets are working as digital content leaders, digital news producers, digital directors, and more.

Attendees of the ONA conference included the *Tribune Media*'s Vice President of Digital, the Digital Director for *La Nacion*, the Director of Digital Innovation at *The Associated Press*, *The New York Times*'s Senior Editor of Digital Storytelling, and the Senior Platform Editor for Digital for the *Wall Street Journal*.

Nearly 100 participants held job titles such as social media producer, social media editor, and social media manager. Another 100 had the role of audience engagement editor, producer, and director.

In the majority of the jobs listed above, understanding how to optimize content for mobile and social media is a huge part of the role.

Even smaller, more local newspapers are looking for those with social media skills. For example, one September 2018 job posting read, "The Statesville (N.C.) Record & Landmark, a daily newspaper covering Iredell County, immediately north of the Charlotte metro area, is looking for a multimedia journalist to join its award-winning staff. The ideal candidate will have solid reporting and photography skills, and the ability to use social media to push content quickly and effectively to a wider audience."[11]

"Content analyses of news media job advertisements have demonstrated the industry's interest in hiring digitally competent employees," Dr. Stephanie E. Bor wrote in her 2014 article, *Teaching Social Media Journalism: Challenges and Opportunities for Future Curriculum Design.* "While theoretical knowledge and basic writing and communication skills remain top requirements," she continued, "employers are also requesting that applicants possess skills in web content creation, multiplatform adaptability, and social media."[12]

So, what does this mean for today's journalist?

"Often, the introduction of new technology into the media sphere has caused disruption, chaos, and bells tolling the end times of journalism," Emory Paine wrote in his honors thesis, *The Next Step: Social Media and the Evolution of Journalism.* "And, each time, the news survived. Indeed, by swiftly converging with the new mediums and incorporating their values into journalism, the news did more than survive – it evolved. Social media represents the next occurrence of this cycle."[13]

This book is divided into two parts.

Part I explores several theoretical frameworks to understand the impact of social media on journalism, and how the relationship between news media and audience has changed because of advances in technologies and changes in consumer behavior.

Part II offers a step-by-step guide to acquiring the skills necessary to navigate in this new media landscape.

Notes

1 Read, Write and Think, http://www.readwritethink.org/classroom-resources/calendar-activities/york-times-used-slogan-20412.html, accessed May 14, 2018.
2 2017 Gallup/Knight Foundation Survey on Trust, Media and Democracy, https://knightfoundation.org/reports/american-views-trust-media-and-democracy, accessed May 14, 2018.
3 Pew Research Center, May 9, 2017, http://www.journalism.org/2017/05/10/americans-attitudes-about-the-news-media-deeply-divided-along-partisan-lines/pj_2017-05-10_media-attitudes_a-05/, accessed May 14, 2018.

4 2017 Gallup/Knight Foundation Survey on Trust, Media and Democracy, https://knightfoundation.org/reports/american-views-trust-media-and-democracy, accessed May 14, 2018.

5 Cheney Thomas, "The development of journalism in the face of social media," University of Gothenburg Department of Applied Information Technology Gothenburg, Sweden, August 2013, Report No. 2013:115 ISSN: 1651-4769, https://gupea.ub.gu.se/bitstream/2077/33941/1/gupea_2077_33941_1.pdf

6 Jeffrey Gottfried and Elisa Shearer, "Americans' online news use is closing in on TV news use," September 7, 2017, Pew Research Center, http://www.pewresearch.org/fact-tank/2017/09/07/americans-online-news-use-vs-tv-news-use/, accessed May 15, 2018.

7 Katerina Eva Matsa, "Fewer Americans rely on TV news; what type they watch varies by who they are," January 5, 2018, Pew Research Center, http://www.pewresearch.org/fact-tank/2018/01/05/fewer-americans-rely-on-tv-news-what-type-they-watch-varies-by-who-they-are/, accessed September 10, 2018.

8 Elizabeth Grieco, "More Americans are turning to multiple social media sites for news," November 7, 2017, Pew Research Center, http://www.pewresearch.org/fact-tank/2017/11/02/more-americans-are-turning-to-multiple-social-media-sites-for-news/, accessed May 14, 2018.

9 Edelman Trust Barometer, https://www.edelman.co.uk/magazine/posts/edelman-trust-barometer-2018/, accessed May 14, 2018.

10 Ibid.

11 Google Jobs, https://www.google.com/search?q=digital+journalist+jobs&ibp=htl;jobs&rciv=jb&clksrc=alertsemail&hl=en&gl=US#fpstate=tldetail&htichips=date_posted:range_2018-09-10&htidocid=KYT51-jcMtfUMdU2 AAAAAA%3D%3D&htiq=digital%20journalist%20jobs&htischips=date_posted;range_2018-09-10&htivrt=jobs, accessed September 10, 2018.

12 Stephanie E. Bor, "Teaching Social Media Journalism: Challenges and Opportunities for Future Curriculum Design," *Journalism & Mass Communication Educator*, vol. 69, no. 3, pp. 243–255, September 2014, https://search-proquest-com.jpllnet.sfsu.edu/docview/1559860258?accountid=13802, accessed May 14, 2018.

13 Emory Paine, "The Next Step: Social Media and the Evolution of Journalism," Salem State Univerity, https://digitalcommons.salemstate.edu/cgi/viewcontent.cgi?article=1052&context=honors_theses, accessed September 7, 2018.

Part I

History and Overview of the Evolution of Social Media in Journalism

1 A Theoretical Framework for Understanding the Impact and Role of Social Media in Journalism

In the **Information Age**, communication, defined as the act of exchanging information by speaking, writing, or using some other medium,[1] has exploded. People from all over the world – no longer confined by geography, economics, or even language – are discussing politics, sharing selfies, and even starting movements.

The most basic communication theory states that communication consists of a sender, a message, a channel where the message travels, noise or interference, and a receiver.[2]

In the very early years of American history, the primary channel through which information traveled was the newspaper, the owners of newspapers – "wealthy administrators of the English crown"[3] – were the "senders" and the subscribers or readers were the "receivers."

Under the **Four Theories of the Press model**,[4] the type of journalism practiced by the wealthy administrators is perhaps best described as falling under the **Authoritarian Theory**, which meant that the mass media had as much freedom as the leadership would permit.[5]

As colonists sought their independence from Great Britain, newsletters and papers such as Thomas Paine's *Common Sense* proliferated, becoming a key method of galvanizing the masses in the years leading up to the American Revolution. After winning independence, American news entities began to practice journalism under the **Libertarian Theory**, which stated that interference from kings or governors should be restrained.[6] The Libertarian Theory also stated that the mass media was to be privately owned and the theory prioritized freedom of thought and individualism.

After independence, newspapers that fell along party lines grew quickly – thanks to the U.S. Constitution guaranteeing freedom of the press and subsidies from the U.S. Postal Service.

In the 1830s, newspapers became less partisan and cheaper, selling for as little as a penny. This allowed people from different political leanings and economic levels to enjoy the same publications – and it allowed publishers to reach a mass audience. But most of the owners, publishers, and editors at these newspapers were often white, wealthy men, and this limited group decided what the news was for the mass audience.

Under the **Gatekeeping Theory**, these owners were considered the gatekeepers of news and information for the general public.

The **gatekeeper** decides "what information should move to group or individual and what information should not. Here, the gatekeeper are the decision makers who letting the whole social system. The gatekeeper is having its own influence like social, cultural, ethical and political. Based on personal or social influences they let the information to the group."[7]

Even after the arrival of radio in 1920 and television in 1940, the news media largely dictated what was most important. Station and network owners, reporters and producers were again mostly white, generally affluent, and college educated. They decided what information the majority of Americans was exposed to.

"With the rise of the Internet era, traditional news faced many challenges in transmitting the messages to their audiences," according to Cheney Thomas' 2013 thesis for the University of Gothenburg in Sweden. "This change in delivering news to certain target groups brought about a transformation from the top-down model of journalism, with writers as gatekeepers of information, to a decentralized system where users have a more active role in the formation of news."[8]

The people who owned or worked at these newspapers and broadcast stations were considered the gatekeepers of news and other information vital to the public. As news companies began to conglomerate – buy up multiple newspapers, magazines, TV, and/or radio stations – the public began to question whether all the news "fit to print" was meant for the public or a select few.

"There is another sector of the media, the elite media, sometimes called the agenda-setting media because they are the ones with the big resources, they set the framework in which everyone else operates," wrote Noam Chomsky in his 1997 article, "What Makes Mainstream Media Mainstream." "*The New York Times* and CBS, that kind of thing. Their audience is mostly privileged people. The people who read the *New York Times*—people who are wealthy or part of what is sometimes called the political class—they are actually involved in the political system in an ongoing fashion."[9]

The **Agenda-Setting Theory** states that in "choosing and displaying news, editors, newsroom staff, and broadcasters play an important part in shaping political reality. Readers learn not only about a given issue, but also how much importance to attach to that issue from the amount of information in a news story and its position. In reflecting what candidates are saying during a campaign, the mass media may well determine the important issues—that is, the media may set the 'agenda' of the campaign."[10]

Even though the role of the news media was considered vital to public discourse, many in the news business did not shy away from racy headlines, revealing photos, and other sensationalized news stories as a way to gain audience share. As publishers fought to attract more readers and broadcasters sought to steal listeners and viewers away from other stations, sensationalism, defined as "the act of foregoing accuracy or dignity in order to capture headlines or public attention,"[11] skyrocketed.

By World War II, public outcry over elitism, sensationalism, and media conglomeration prompted a small group of powerful journalist and educators to form the **Hutchins Commission**. Worried that the freedom of the press was in danger, the commission came up with five recommendations[12] to address the public's concerns:

(1) truthful, comprehensive, and intelligent account of the day's events;
(2) a forum for the exchange of comment and criticism;
(3) the projection of a representative picture of the constituent groups in the society;
(4) the presentation and clarification of the goals and values of the society;
(5) full access to the day's intelligence.

These recommendations initially met with resistance within the media industry, but over time many companies and individuals embraced these principles, adopting ethical guidelines and policies that are relied upon by journalists and journalism schools to this day.

Through self-regulation, media companies were able to avoid more public outcry and possible government interference, preserving the freedom of the press, which had been written into the U.S. Constitution at a time when technology was not seen as a threat. During this era, journalists sought to be impartial, detached, balanced, and accurate in their reporting of news, which many scholars have referred to as the **objectivity norm**."

"The objectivity norm guides journalists to separate facts from values and to report only the facts. Objective reporting is supposed to be cool, rather than emotional, in tone," wrote Michael Schudson in *The Objectivity Norm in American Journalism*. "Objective reporting takes pains to represent fairly each leading side in a political controversy."[13]

Although critics have argued that objectivity is impossible to achieve, the concept had been held as a cornerstone of American journalism,[14] and trust in the news media reached an all-time high in 1976 at 72 percent, according to a recent Gallup poll.[15]

"Over the history of the entire trend, Americans' trust and confidence hit its highest point in 1976, at 72 percent, in the wake of widely lauded examples of investigative journalism regarding Vietnam and the Watergate scandal," wrote Gallup poll reporter Art Swift. "After staying in the low to mid-50s through the late 1990s and into the early years of the new century, Americans' trust in the media has fallen slowly and steadily. It has consistently been below a majority level since 2007."[16]

In the last few years, trust in the news media is starting to strengthen, especially in light of the recent problems with fake news popping up on various social media platforms. This is good news for those who believe that journalism holds a special responsibility as the **Fourth Estate**, which essentially means the public relies on the press to monitor government and expose wrongdoing.[17]

Even so, the power that the news media held as the most powerful gate-keepers or agenda-setters in the United States may never go back to what it used to be. That's because the relationship between the sender (the news media) and the receiver (the public) has changed, thanks to the world wide web, advances in technology, and the affordability of and easy access to mobile devices.

Nowadays, the consumer has the power to choose when, where, and how to learn which team won the game, where the earthquake struck, if the president held a meeting with North Korea – all through the power of the Internet and social media.

In addition, thousands of people with no formal training or experience in journalism are deciding to produce their own version of news: sharing text, pictures, and video that often **scoop** the mainstream media outlets. Those who post stories regularly have built a sizable group of followers, thus becoming **citizen journalists**.

Citizen journalism, according to *Encyclopedia Britannica*, is conducted by people who are not professional journalists but disseminate information around the world. And it has expanded worldwide, with people in disaster

Marques Brownlee ✓
@MKBHD

Web Video Producer | ⋈ | Pro Ultimate
Frisbee Player

Figure 1.1 Marques Brownlee bio on Twitter as of Nov. 4, 2018. Twitter.

Figure 1.2 A review of a new product from Marques Brownlee. Twitter.

zones providing live or on-the-scene information that no one else has. "People in countries affected by political upheaval and often in countries where print and broadcast media are controlled by the government have used a variety of technological tools to share information about hot spots."[18]

Marques Brownlee, noted by *The Guardian* back in 2014 as one of the "top 30 young people in digital media,"[19] now has more than six million people following his tech news on YouTube and three million followers on Twitter.

Reni Eddo-Lodge, who also made *The Guardian* list, has a podcast about race. She now has a following of nearly 50,000 people on Twitter.[20]

Tavi Gevinson, also recognized by *The Guardian* for creating her own site on style, "Rookie," now has nearly 400,000 followers on Twitter and more than 252,000 followers on Instagram. Tavi is among a newer generation of bloggers and entrepreneurs who are finding their voice and audience through the power of social media.

In the mid-2000s, instant messengers and social media networks such as Facebook became the newest channels for communication, making it even easier for citizens to play journalist (sharing photos and stories about war, unrest, and other issues important to the public) with the simple click of a button on their smartphone or computer. The public, through social acts of liking, commenting, and re-posting stories, became just as important as editors and publishers in deciding the top news stories of the day.

Figure 1.3 Bio of Reni Eddo-Lodge on Twitter as of Nov. 4, 2018. Twitter.

Figure 1.4 Tavi Gevinson's Instagram bio as of Nov. 4, 2018. Twitter.

The public no longer had to wait for the 5 o'clock news or the morning paper to find out what was happening in their communities or anywhere in the world. Twitter, Snapchat (as of 2011), and other social networks made it possible for almost anyone to share their stories, views, images, and videos with others, and each network's powerful algorithm makes it possible for one tweet or post to go **viral** (or reach millions or billions of people).

As new channels of communication opened, businesses, marketers, publicists, and special interest groups began to share their own content, some in the form of news. In some cases, these news stories were thinly veiled ads or political propaganda. Others were skewed; some were outright fake. Consumers, however, initially had no way of knowing what was produced by independent journalists following the tradition of fairness of 20th-century journalists.

The reason? Many social networks were born out of the idea that information should flow freely between people. Founders of these networks often lauded social media as a way to even the playing field, which many had complained had been dominated by people who were out of touch with everyday people.

According to marketing specialist Dominick Damico, "It wasn't until the web came along (and with it, social media) did we see the true democratization of influence. Platforms like Twitch, YouTube, Facebook, Instagram, and Snapchat put the power to create in the hands of the people."[21]

While there is evidence to suggest that a growing number of young people are leaving Facebook, [22] Pew Research Center reported that 45 percent of Americans using Facebook said they got their news on the social network in 2017.[23] And 74 percent of American Twitter users said they got their news from the platform. On YouTube, 32 percent used the platform for news and nearly 30 percent of Snapchat users said they got news from the mobile application.[24]

While social media executives continue to reject the label of news media company, Bill Kovach and Tom Rosenstiel, in *The Elements of Journalism*, note that the purpose of journalism "is not defined by technology, nor by the journalists or the techniques they employ. The principles and purposes of journalism are defined by something more basic; the function news plays in the lives of people."[25]

Thus, social media networks – for better or worse – have become some of the channels where receivers (the audience) seek news, and under the Gatekeeping Theory, they can be considered among today's news gatekeepers, not just as drivers to more traditional news sites but as originators of news.

Philip M. Napoli, in his article "Social Media and the Public Interest: Governance of News Platforms in the Realm of Individual and Algorithmic Gatekeepers," wrote that "Social media platforms also can serve as important mechanisms via which news is initially generated and disseminated into the broader media ecosystem . . . That is, social media need not only serve to relay news from other news outlets; these platforms can serve as the originating source as well."[26]

Even so, many critics say people sharing tweets or posts on Facebook does not equate to journalism.

"Information is not journalism," Richard Sambrook, the director of the *BBC Global News* division, told *The Guardian*. "You get a lot of things, when you open up Twitter in the morning, but not journalism. Journalism needs discipline, analysis, explanation and context, he pointed out, and therefore for him it is still a profession. The value that gets added with journalism is judgment, analysis and explanation – and that makes the difference."[27]

There is quite a bit of truth to that. Indeed, the number of people paying for digital subscriptions to traditional news outlets is steadily rising, especially now that many networks and newspapers have adopted a **Digital First** newsroom.

The concept of Digital First has been around for years. As defined by media observer Jeff Jarvis, in his 2011 article for *The Guardian*,

> Going digital does not mean merely putting articles online before the presses roll, as then print still rules the process. No – digital first means the net must drive all decisions: how news is covered, in what form, by whom, and when. It dictates that when journalists know something, they are prepared to share it with their public. They may share what they know before their knowledge is complete so the public can help fill in blanks.
>
> In this way, digital first resets the journalistic relationship with the community, making the news organization less a producer and more an open platform for the public to share what it knows.
>
> It is to that process that the journalist adds value. She may do so in many forms – reporting, curating people and their information, providing applications and tools, gathering data, organizing effort, educating participants . . . and writing articles.[28]

Thus, while the platforms are the means by which people might find out about a news story, the actual story still comes from mainstream or emerging news outlets dedicated to fair and balanced reporting. Although truth may vary based on perspective, numerous news outlets are gaining a digital audience – by using social media as part of their editorial strategy.

This book focuses on how journalists from small, large, and startup news outlets can use social media to engage in the new way of communicating with their audience. Today, the audience is as important as journalists in deciding what the news is. This "new" relationship might be best understood under the Uses and Gratification Theory (UGT),[29] which "differs from other media effect theories in that it assumes that individuals have power over their media usage, rather than positioning individuals as passive consumers of media."[30]

The UGT, which some have noted in relation to **Maslow's Hierarchy of Needs**,[31] explores how individuals seek out all types of media to fulfill five different needs: the need for information and education, entertainment, personal identity, social interaction, and escapism.[32]

Conclusion

According to the Learning Theories website, "Today, UGT has more relevance than ever as a tool for understanding how we as individuals connect with the technologies around us. These technologies span everything from the Internet to video gaming to mobile phones. UGT research into mobile phone usage has found that people seek a number of gratifications from their phones, including affection/sociability, entertainment, and mobility, among others."[33]

While this theory does not explore how the mass media affects the audience, it assumes that the audience chooses to engage with media for different reasons. In various chapters of this book, we'll examine how the UGT Theory can help journalists reach their target audience.

Discussion Questions

1   What would you do if you gave up media for one day? Do you think we should do this? Why or why not?
2   What type of media educates the public? Please explain why.
3   How does UGT differ from the Agenda-setting Theory?
4   How does the Gatekeeping Theory differ from the Agenda-setting Theory?
5   Name a few video games that allow you to escape reality? Why do they enable you to escape?
6   In what ways do you think social media has improved journalism?
7   Which theories best describe the role of the traditional news media during the 1900s? Please explain.

Exercises

Please watch the video on the Uses and Gratification Theory and answer the following questions:

1   Does television educate, according to the video?
2   Do we learn and mimic the behavior of characters we see on TV?
3   Define reception theory.
4   Which category does reality TV fit into?

You can find the video by going to this link: https://revision-world.com/a2-level-level-revision/media-studies-level-revision/uses-and-gratifications-theory.

Notes

1 Online version of *Oxford Dictionary*, definition of communication, https://en.oxforddictionaries.com/definition/communication, accessed December 28, 2017.

2 Shannon and Weaver, Chapter 1: Communication Theory, in *Introduction to Communication Studies* [e-book]. Taylor & Francis Ltd / Books, 1990, pp. 6–23. Available from: Communication & Mass Media Complete, Ipswich, Mass. http://www.oxfordreference.com/view/10.1093/oi/authority.20110803100459436, accessed January 3, 2018.

3 Journalism in the Digital Age website, https://cs.stanford.edu/people/eroberts/cs181/projects/2010-11/Journalism/index8067.html?page_id=14, accessed on December 31, 2017.

4 Maira T. Vaca-Baqueiro, *Four Theories of the Press: 60 Years and Counting*. London, Routledge, 2018.

5 Fred S. Siebert, Theodore Peterson, and Wilbur Schramm, *Four Theories of the Press: The Authoritarian, Libertarian, Social Responsibility, and Soviet Communist Concepts of What the Press Should Be and Do*. Urbana, Ill., Univ. of Illinois Press, 1956.

6 Ibid.

7 Communication Theory website, https://www.communicationtheory.org/gatekeeping-theory/, accessed May 18, 2018.

8 Cheney Thomas, "The development of journalism in the face of social media," University of Gothenburg Department of Applied Information Technology Gothenburg, Sweden, August 2013, Report No. 2013:115 ISSN: 1651-4769, https://gupea.ub.gu.se/bitstream/2077/33941/1/gupea_2077_33941_1.pdf

9 Noam Chomsky, "What Makes Mainstream Media Mainstream," *Z Magazine*, https://chomsky.info/199710__/, accessed May 18, 2018.

10 Maxwell E. McCombs and Donald L. Shaw, "The Agenda-Setting Function of Mass Media," *Public Opinion Quarterly*, vol. 36, no. 2, January 1, 1972, https://doi.org/10.1086/267990

11 Comm455/History of Journalism, http://historyofjournalism.onmason.com/2012/09/25/sensationalism-in-america/, accessed May 14, 2018.

12 Ibid.

13 Michael Schudson, "The Objectivity Norm in American Journalism*." *Journalism*, vol. 2, no. 2, 2001, pp. 149–170.

14 Jayeon Lee, "The Double-Edged Sword: The Effects of Journalists' Social Media Activities on Audience Perceptions of Journalists and Their News Products." *Journal of Computer-Mediated Communication*, vol. 20, no. 3, 2015, pp. 312–329.

15 Art Swift, "Americans' trust in mass media sinks to an all-time low," Gallup, September 14, 2016, http://news.gallup.com/poll/195542/americans-trust-mass-media-sinks-new-low.aspx, accessed May 18, 2018.

16 Ibid.

17 Julia Petley, "Fourth Rate Estate," *Index on Censorship*, vol. 33, April 1, 2004, https://doi-org.jpllnet.sfsu.edu/10.1080/03064220408537330, accessed May 18, 2018.

18 *Encyclopedia Britannica*, https://www.britannica.com/topic/citizen-journalism.

19 "The top 30 young people in digital media," *The Guardian*, March 16, 2014, https://www.theguardian.com/media/2014/mar/16/top-30-young-people-digital-media-nos-30-11

20 "About Race" podcast by Reni Eddo-Lodge, https://www.aboutracepodcast.com/, accessed July 7, 2018.

21 Dominick Damic, "Social media and the democratization of influence," Adspire, http://adspiresocial.com/social-media-democratization-influence/, accessed July 15, 2018.

22 Andrew Perrin, "Americans are changing their relationship with Facebook," Pew Research Center, September 5, 2018, http://www.pewresearch.org/fact-tank/2018/09/05/americans-are-changing-their-relationship-with-facebook/, accessed September 8, 2018.

23 Jeffrey Gottfried and Elisa Shearer, *News Use Across Social Media Platforms 2017*, Pew Research Center, September 7, 2017, http://www.journalism.org/2017/09/07/news-use-across-social-media-platforms-2017/, accessed on February 1, 2018.

24 Ibid.

25 Bill Kovach and Tom Rosenstiel. *The Elements of Journalism: What Newspeople Should Know and the Public Should Expect*. Completely Updated and Revised. ed., 2014.

26 Philip M. Napoli, "Social Media and the Public Interest: Governance of News Platforms in the Realm of Individual and Algorithmic Gatekeepers," *Telecommunications Policy* vol. 39, no. 9, 2015, pp. 751–760, a https://doi.org/10.1016/j.telpol.2014.12.003, accessed June 1, 2018.

27 Mercedes Bunz, "How Social Networking is Changing Journalism," September 18, 2009, *The Guardian*, https://www.theguardian.com/media/pda/2009/sep/18/oxford-social-media-convention-2009-journalism-blogs, accessed June 1, 2018.

28 Jeff Jarvis, "Digital first: what it means for journalism," *The Guardian*, June 26, 2011, https://www.theguardian.com/media/2011/jun/26/digital-first-what-means-journalism, accessed August 25, 2018.

29 *Learning Theories*, https://www.learning-theories.com/uses-and-gratification-theory.html, accessed May 14, 2018.

30 Ibid.

31 *Businesstopia*, https://www.businesstopia.net/mass-communication/uses-gratifications-theory, accessed May 14, 2018.

32 *Revision World*, https://revisionworld.com/a2-level-level-revision/media-studies-level-revision/uses-and-gratifications-theory, accessed March 25, 2019.

33 *Learning Theories*, https://www.learning-theories.com/uses-and-gratification-theory.html

2 The Evolution of Social Media in Journalism

In the 1990s, instant messengers, such as ICQ, MSN, AIM, and Yahoo! Messenger,[1] were among the first wave of social media, allowing their users to create online communities to share information, ideas, personal messages, and other content.[2]

In 1997, Six Degrees became the first social networking site by combining "personal profiles, instant messaging, friend lists and the ability to search other members' friends lists."[3] At its peak, the site had one million users.[4] It was based on the theory that "everyone is six or fewer steps away, by way of introduction, from any other person in the world, so that a chain of 'a friend of a friend' statements can be made to connect any two people in a maximum of six steps."[5]

Though it lasted only four years, Six Degrees became a predecessor for Friendster, MySpace, Facebook, LinkedIn, and many other social networking sites based on the concept of "social circles," or connecting with people who held some connection to your friends, family, and colleagues.

Indeed, Facebook, which launched in 2004, has said it believes that everyone in the world is connected to "every other person by an average of three and a half people."[6] The concept is similar for LinkedIn, launched in 2003, which identifies the second- and third-degree connections of each member.

LinkedIn is one of the many social networks that were able to build a global membership base by encouraging members to continue building their network by connecting with people beyond their immediate friends or family. LinkedIn, which reached nearly 600 million members in 2018, sought to set itself apart from Facebook by calling itself a professional network, where members connected with like-minded professionals for business opportunities and jobs.

In the earlier versions of Facebook, LinkedIn, and some other social networking sites, members communicated by sending messages to one another. This one-to-one communication method was a chief reason why social media, including instant messengers, was considered different from print or broadcast media, which had the power to transmit a message to a mass audience.

Thus, the early versions of social networking sites were not seen as a direct threat to media outlets. Indeed, online news sites and news aggregators were seen as bigger threats in the early years.[7]

By the early 2000s, social media, including instant messengers, began to shift from one-to-one communication to one-to-many. In 2000, an instant messaging system called Jabber[8] launched, acting as a "single gateway for users to chat with friends and access their buddy lists on all of the big networks at the time: AIM, Yahoo and MSN."[9] Apple created iChat in 2002 and Skype was founded in 2003, allowing users to communicate with others through video, voice, and instant messaging. Meebo began as an instant messaging service in 2005 and was eventually acquired in 2011 by Google.

In July 2006, Twitter arrived, introducing a newsfeed that could be seen by anyone and everyone. Twitter allowed users to choose whether to share tweets only with mutual followers, by "protecting" them, or make them public to the world. The concept was similar to Flickr, an online photo management and sharing application[10] that was created in 2004 and acquired by Yahoo in 2005.[11]

Unlike the "six degrees" concept of connecting with friends, family, and people you know, Twitter allowed members to choose who to follow based on their content – similar to the way consumers chose to subscribe to a particular magazine or tune into a certain program.

This concept was not that different from Digg,[12] a social networking site founded in 2004. Digg, billed as a social news site because it allowed members to submit and share blogs and other content, was quickly followed by Reddit, whose name plays on the words, "read it," in 2005. Billed as a "social news site," Reddit gave members the power to decide what the top stories of the day were by allowing members to vote up or down on content.

In September 2006, Facebook introduced "an algorithmically generated and constantly refreshing summary of updates about the activities of one's friends."[13] Despite the fact that the news feed is now a standard part of nearly every social networking site, many Facebook members initially protested the news feed, calling it "overwhelming" and "cluttered." And some went so far as to demand its removal, likening the news feed to "stalking."[14]

Mark Zuckerberg acknowledged those early users' concerns but insisted that the news feed was here to stay. "We're not oblivious of the Facebook groups popping up about this (by the way, [our news feed product manager] is not the devil)," he said in an article in Mashable. "And we agree, stalking isn't cool; but being able to know what's going on in your friends' lives is . . . This is information people used to dig for on a daily basis, nicely reorganized and summarized so people can learn about the people they care about."[15]

Within a very short time, most other networks followed suit, allowing members the power to choose to make their news feed, or even certain posts, public or private. In 2007, Tumblr, a microblogging and social networking site for multimedia and short posts, launched, and it now hosts more than 356 million blogs[16] and has more than 725 million monthly unique visitors worldwide.[17] Thus, the newsfeed gave the average user the power to attract an audience. This meant that social media could become a purveyor of news and information, much like broadcast and print media.

"For instance, the news about the death of Michael Jackson in 2009, Facebook and Twitter users broke the story ahead of any major news network, the moment the UCLA Medical Center made the death announcement official," Jennifer Alejandro wrote in her 2010 Reuters Institute paper. "Social network sites, search engines and news websites reported heavy traffic volumes in the hour the story broke and some websites even crashed. That single story showed how news is consumed and disseminated in social media, how far it can reach and how fast."[18]

By December 2009, global users were spending "more than five and a half hours on social networking sites."[19] In the United States, time spent on social networking sites continues to rise with the heaviest users being Generation X (Gen X), people aged 35 to 49. According to the 2016 Nielsen Social Media Report, Gen Xers spend "almost seven hours per week versus Millennials, who come in second, spending just over six hours per week."[20]

With huge advances in technology, including the ease and affordability of using smartphones and other mobile devices, social networking sites evolved from a text-centric platform to one that featured a wide array of visual content, which is more than 40 times more likely to get shared on social media than other types of content.[21]

Blogging, which took off in the 1990s and is often characterized by the need to reveal one's own opinion on issues of the day,[22] has also evolved, with many social networks incorporating easy-to-use publishing platforms into their sites.

In 2012, two co-founders of Twitter launched Medium, an online publishing platform. Like Twitter, Medium encouraged users to post content and develop a following based on content. Unlike Twitter, users didn't have to worry about a 140-word character limit.

Medium is viewed by many as a form of social journalism because it consists of a "hybrid of professional journalism, contributor and reader content."[23] Twitter co-founder Ev Williams, who helped launched Medium, says the new platform is certainly that – and more.

Williams wrote in his 2012 post announcing the arrival of Medium:

> In 1999, two friends and I launched Blogger, a simple tool for publishing on the web. Blogs, or 'weblogs,' were largely unknown outside a small community of web geeks. The idea that anyone, anywhere, could publish for a global audience seemed radical.

Today, we carry the Internet around on pocket-sized devices with more computing power and pixels than we previously had on our desks a few years ago. We have innumerable options for sharing our deep thoughts or cat photos—with or without a retro filter. Our collective, casual, everyday shares demonstrate that millions of people have the power of a printing press at their fingertips. (And they use it.) That is an amazing advancement.

We think there's more to do.[24]

Also, in 2012, Twitter acquired Vine, a social network that allowed members to post six-second videos. Vine's videos were done by amateurs who often engaged others through slapstick humor, but, like Twitter, it was based on the concept of connection based on content that could be seen by anyone and everyone.

Vine was so popular with teenagers and 20-somethings that many young people were able to develop a huge following of fans from all over the world. A number of these "Vine Famous" people went onto television stardom; some earned money and gifts through endorsements. Though Vine was considered a hit among young people, Twitter shut it down in 2016.[25] Many of those who attained fame on Vine continue to create content and attract an audience on other social networking sites, such as Facebook, Instagram, and YouTube.

Enter Snapchat. With all the pizazz and quirkiness of Vine, combined with the power of one-to-one communication, Snapchat has become the social network du jour. Many college students use it to share their latest meal, or their favourite outfit, to only their closest friends or just one friend.

Launched in 2011 by three students at Stanford University, Snapchat allows users to send a photo or video that lasts up to 10 seconds. The receiver of that message can take a screenshot of the image before it disappears. Because of Snapchat's popularity with younger people, many companies, including media companies, have also started to share branded messages and news stories on the site.

YouTube, which launched in 2005, has an open-access model that has allowed many people to share content with the masses, thereby becoming "YouTube famous." YouTube is considered the second biggest social networking site after Facebook,[26] garnering about 30 million visitors per day. An estimated eight out of ten people between the ages of 18 to 49 watch YouTube each month.[27] Indeed, YouTube and other video streaming sites have become so popular that it is predicted that half of viewers under the age of 32 will not subscribe to pay-TV services by 2025.[28]

Instagram, created in 2010 and bought for $1 billion[29] by Facebook in 2012, also allows its 700 million members to publicly showcase their work, and grow the number of followers based on their content. The site, however, additionally enables members to remain private, and even engage in one-to-one communication through direct messages. Many people once famous on Vine can now be found on Instagram, which features videos up to 60 seconds long.

Video is arguably the king of content at the moment, and mobile video in particular is expected to account for 75 percent of the total mobile data traffic by 2020. One social networking platform that is taking full advantage of this trend is Snapchat, which has more than 166 million daily active users.[30] Recent data shows that Snapchat users were watching ten billion videos per day, up from eight billion in just two months.[31]

In addition, Twitter, Facebook, Instagram, and other social networking sites now allow and encourage members to post "live" video, meaning that a user can record video in real time, and broadcast it to one or many. Even journalists are using the "live" aspect of these social networking sites to share news and information. Instant messengers continue to rise in popularity as well. Facebook Messenger, launched in in 2011, is one of the biggest instant messengers in the world with more than one billion members.[32] WhatsApp is the other big instant messenger with an equally large membership.[33]

Thus, the traditional paradigm of social networking sites and instant messengers as places for the exchange of messages through private conversations among friends, family, and acquaintances has shifted dramatically. Under the UGT, the audience is turning to social media, often from their mobile devices, to acquire knowledge and understanding.

Indeed, the latest research shows that social networking sites have become a key source of information for many consumers. In the United States, the majority of Twitter and Facebook users rely on "each platform serv[ing] as a source for news about events and issues outside the realm of friends and family," according to a Pew Research Center survey of 2,000 people in March 2015. That share, the study found, has increased substantially from 2013, when about half of users (52 percent of Twitter users, 47 percent of Facebook users) said they got news from the social platforms. The Pew survey also found that the rise of users getting news from their news feeds "cuts across nearly every demographic group."[34]

Even journalists are getting their news from social media. A Cision survey found that more than half of the 1.5 million journalists and influencers interviewed said they could not work without social media.[35]

In the United Kingdom, a study from Canterbury Christ Church University and Cision found that social media is now an "everyday tool for the media with 96 percent of UK journalists using it on a daily basis."[36] The survey also found that 42 percent of UK journalists say that they would "not be able to carry out their work without social media."

"All big news organizations are plunging into the world of social media, looking at its extraordinary newsgathering potential; its potential as a new tool to engage the audience; and as a way of distributing our news," Kevin Bakhurst of the BBC said in 2011 during a speech given to the International Broadcasting Convention in Amsterdam.[37]

Journalists, however, are not the only people sharing news via social media.

On June 13, 2009, millions of people in Iran protested on the streets and on Twitter after learning that incumbent Mahmoud Ahmadinejad had won more than 66 percent of the vote against popular opposition candidate Mir-Hossein Mousavi. As the Iranian government moved to suppress the protests, both on- and offline, Twitter delivered information in real time.

Less than a week after the Iranian protests, Journalist Lev Grossman surmised that Twitter's ability to broadcast the news far and wide made it "practically ideal for a mass protest movement, both very easy for the average citizen to use and very hard for any central authority to control."[38]

Grossman also called Twitter the "medium of the moment."

> It's free, highly mobile, very personal and very quick. It's also built to spread, and fast. Twitterers like to append notes called hashtags — #theylooklikethis — to their tweets, so that they can be grouped and searched for by topic; especially interesting or urgent tweets tend to get picked up and retransmitted by other Twitterers, a practice known as retweeting, or just RT. And Twitter is promiscuous by nature: tweets go out over two networks, the Internet and SMS, the network that cell phones use for text messages, and they can be received and read on practically anything with a screen and a network connection.[39]

Thus, citizens have become journalists, giving rise to the term, "citizen journalism" or "participatory journalism."

"The Internet gave average people the ability to transmit information globally," veteran journalist Tony Rogers wrote in a 2016 blog post for

Figure 2.1 Screenshot of Melissa Mackenzie's tweet during 2009 presidential election in Iran. Twitter.

Figure 2.2 Screenshot of Iranian student's June 16, 2009 tweet following 2009
          presidential election. Twitter.

Figure 2.3 Screenshot of President Trump's Nov. 2, 2008 tweet announcing the
          U.S. added 250,000 jobs in October. Twitter.

ThoughtCo.com. "That was a power once reserved for only the very largest
media corporations and news agencies."[40]

During the 2016 presidential election in the United States, President
Donald Trump, who was then a candidate, often took his message straight
to the "Twitterverse," bypassing news conferences, press releases, and other
traditional methods that politicians traditionally used to communicate with
the news media.

"(Howard) Dean revolutionized online fundraising in 2004," NPR
reporter Sam Sanders wrote in a 2016 analysis. "Obama took grassroots
organizing online to a new level in '08. And this election's tech breakthrough might be Donald Trump's ability to capture the world's attention
on a regular basis with just a tweet."[41]

Trump continues to "capture the world's attention" as president of the
United States, often taking to Twitter in the early hours of the morning,
prompting journalists to rely on Twitter and other social networks even
more than before.

Conclusion

Even before Trump, President Barack Obama had become the most
followed politician on Twitter, with 102 million followers. As of April

2019, Trump had nearly 60 million followers. In addition, numerous law enforcement and government agencies now post many of their announcements on Twitter and several other social networks. These networks also have become the new telephone books for journalists seeking to diversify their source lists.

Alecia Swasy, the Donald W. Reynolds Chair in Business Journalism at Washington & Lee University and author of *How Journalists Use Twitter: The Changing Landscape of U.S. Newsrooms*, wrote: "One of the most interesting things I found was Twitter's emergence as the new phone directory. Consider the decline of landline telephones, and the subsequent death of the community white pages. A school reporter in Dallas used Twitter to find students and parents by searching keywords on the latest buzz in the schoolyard. As she said: If families do have a landline, teenagers won't answer it, but they're on Twitter chatting about what's going on."[42]

As a result, social media has become an indispensable part of how journalists gather and distribute the news.

"The late 1990s saw the first blogs and web forums; 2004 gave birth to podcasting, where users could create online radio programs; 2005 saw the founding of YouTube, an online video host; and, 2006 saw the worldwide release of Facebook and Twitter, two of the most popular websites today," Emory Paine aptly wrote in his Honors Thesis for Salem State University. "In the eyes of traditional journalism, these social media directly challenged not only their profession, but the very definition of journalism itself."[43]

Discussion Questions

1 Why should journalists use Twitter? How should they stay up on the news?
2 What blogging platform do you remember using first? Do you still use that platform? Why or why not?
3 Do you use instant messengers more than social media to communicate with friends? Why or why not?
4 Do you listen to podcasts more than live radio news programs? If so, why?
5 What was the first social network that you joined? Are you still on that network? Which networks do you like now? Why?
6 Do you think newsrooms should use Snapchat to share their news stories and engage with a younger audience? Why or why not?

Exercises

1   Find three politicians in your local area and list some of their most shared tweets. Explain why you think those posts did well.
2   Look for a Twitter account for your local police department. Review their most recent tweets. Go to the department's website and look for press releases. Note if the police department did a press release on the events or crimes they shared on Twitter.
3   Look for the Facebook account of any U.S. presidents (past or present). What types of information are they sharing on Facebook? Do you think it's useful to journalists? Why or why not?

Notes

1   Matt Petronzio, "A Brief History of Instant Messaging," *Mashable*, October 25, 2012, http://mashable.com/2012/10/25/instant-messaging-history/#Hw2UJ4p. nPqP, last accessed on July 16, 2017.
2   "The Post Social Media Era and the Evolution of Social Networking," http://meshedsociety.com/the-post-social-media-era-and-the-evolution-of-social-networking/, accessed July 7, 2017.
3   Sam Plymale, Eastern Michigan University Public Relations Student Society of American (PRSSA), May 26, 2012, https://emuprssa.com/2012/05/26/a-forefather-of-social-media-andrew-weinreich-and-sixdegrees-com/, accessed on July 11, 2017.
4   Ibid.
5   The Oxford Math Center website, http://www.oxfordmathcenter.com/drupal7/node/655, accessed on July 11, 2017.
6   Smriti Bhagat, Moira Burke, Carlos Diuk, Ismail Onur Filiz, and Sergey Edunov, "Three and a half degrees of separation," February 4, 2016, https://research.fb.com/three-and-a-half-degrees-of-separation/, accessed July 11, 2017.
7   Jennifer Alejandro, "Journalism in the Age of Social Media," Reuters Institute Fellowship Paper, University of Oxford, 2010, https://reutersinstitute.politics.ox.ac.uk/sites/default/files/Journalism%20in%20the%20Age%20of%20Social%20Media.pdf, accessed July 16, 2017.
8   PC Encyclopedia, http://www.pcmag.com/encyclopedia/term/45544/jabber, accessed July 19, 2017
9   Matt Petronzio, "A Brief History of Instant Messaging," *Mashable*, October 25, 2012, http://mashable.com/2012/10/25/instant-messaging-history/#Hw2UJ4p. nPqP, last accessed on July 16, 2017.
10   Flickr About page, https://www.flickr.com/about, accessed on July 16, 2017.
11   Bobbie Johnson, "Facebook patents the 'news feed' – but was it really first?" *The Guardian*, February 26, 2010, https://www.theguardian.com/technology/2010/feb/26/facebook-patent, accessed July 16, 2017.
12   *Digg*, http://digg.com, accessed July 16, 2018.
13   Facebook, "Facebook gets a facelift," Sept. 5, 2006, https://www.facebook.com/notes/facebook/facebook-gets-a-facelift/2207967130/, accessed July 12, 2017.

14 Samantha Murphy, "The Evolution of Facebook News Feed," *Mashable*, March 12, 2013, http://mashable.com/2013/03/12/facebook-news-feed-evolution/#t2w.1X9UBPqD, accessed July 16, 2017.

15 Ibid.

16 Tumblr About page, https://www.tumblr.com/about, accessed July 18, 2017.

17 Statista, "Combined desktop and mobile visits to Tumblr.com from November 2016 to May 2017 (in millions)," https://www.statista.com/statistics/261925/unique-visitors-to-tumblrcom/, accessed July 18, 2017.

18 Ibid.

19 Ibid.

20 Sean Casey, "Nielsen Social, 2016 Social Media Report," January 17, 2017, http://www.nielsen.com/us/en/insights/reports/2017/2016-nielsen-social-media-report.html, accessed on July 16, 2017.

21 Liis Hainla, "21 Social Media Marketing Statistics You Need to Know in 2017," updated June 28, 2017, accessed July 16, 2018. https://www.dreamgrow.com/21-social-media-marketing-statistics/, accessed July 16, 2017.

22 Merriam Webster online site, definition of blog, https://www.merriam-webster.com/dictionary/blog?utm_campaign=sd&utm_medium=serp&utm_source=jsonld, accessed on January 1, 2018.

23 Wikipedia, https://en.wikipedia.org/wiki/Social_journalism, accessed July 19, 2017.

24 Ev Williams, "Welcome to Medium," *Medium*, August 14, 2012, https://medium.com/@ev/welcome-to-medium-9e53ca408c48, accessed August 3, 2018.

25 Chris Foxx, "Twitter axes Vine video service," BBC News, October 27, 2016, http://www.bbc.com/news/technology-37788052, accessed July 12, 2017.

26 Dreamgrow website, "Top 15 most popular social networking sites," https://i1.wp.com/www.dreamgrow.com/wp-content/uploads/2017/05/top-most-popular-social-networking-sites-graph.jpg?ssl=1, last accessed July 19, 2017.

27 FortuneLords, "36 Mind Blowing YouTube Facts, Figures and Statistics – 2017," updated March 23, 2017, https://fortunelords.com/youtube-statistics/, accessed July 15, 2017.

28 Ibid.

29 Salman Aslam, "Instagram by the numbers: stats, demographics & fun facts," June 21, 2017, Omicore, https://www.omnicoreagency.com/instagram-statistics/, last accessed July 15, 2017.

30 CSD, Social Media Statistics, https://chrissniderdesign.com/blog/resources/social-media-statistics/, accessed July 18, 2017.

31 Paul Roberts, "8 Social Media Statistics for 2017," *Our Social Times*, http://oursocialtimes.com/7-social-media-statistics-for-2017/, accessed July 18, 2017.

32 *Pinngle*, "5 Most Popular Messaging Apps of 2017," https://pinngle.me/blog/5-most-popular-messaging-apps-of-2017/, accessed November 4, 2018.

33 Josh Constine, "Facebook now has 2 billion monthly users … and responsibility," June 27, 2017, Tech Crunch, https://techcrunch.com/2017/06/27/facebook-2-billion-users/, accessed July 13, 2017.

34 Pew Research Center, http://www.journalism.org/2015/07/14/the-evolving-role-of-news-on-twitter-and-facebook/, accessed July 16, 2018.

35 Cision website, http://www.prweek.com/article/1354357/infographic-journalists-rely-twitter-pr-sources - pqZ4mwllX4PlyFKL.99, accessed July 11, 2017.

36 Coast Communications, http://www.coastcommunications.co.uk/coastlines/journalists-rely-on-social-media-study-finds.

37   Kevin Bakhurst, "How has social media changed the way newsrooms work?", September 9, 2011, http://www.bbc.co.uk/blogs/theeditors/2011/09/ibc_in_amsterdam.html, accessed July 12, 2017.

38   Lev Grossman, "Iran's Protests: Why Twitter Is the Medium of the Movement," *Time* magazine in partnership with CNN, June 17, 2009, http://content.time.com/time/world/article/0,8599,1905125,00.html, accessed July 14, 2017.

39   Ibid.

40   Tony Rogers, "What is Citizen Journalism," Thoughtco.com, August 30, 2016, https://www.thoughtco.com/what-is-citizen-journalism-2073663, accessed July 12, 2017.

41   "Data Scientists Find Consistencies in Donald Trump's Erratic Twitter Strategy," August 18, 2016, *All Things Considered*, https://www.npr.org/2016/08/18/490523985/data-scientists-find-consistencies-in-donald-trumps-erratic-twitter-strategy, accessed July 10, 2018.

42   Alecia Swasy, "I studied how journalists used Twitter for two years. Here's what I learned," Poynter, March 22, 2017, https://www.poynter.org/news/i-studied-how-journalists-used-twitter-two-years-heres-what-i-learned, accessed August 25, 2018.

43   Emory Paine, "The Next Step: Social Media and the Evolution of Journalism," Salem State University Digital Commons at Salem State University, May 2015, http://digitalcommons.salemstate.edu/cgi/viewcontent.cgi?article=1052&context=honors_theses, accessed on July 12, 2017.

3   Where the Jobs Are

Figure 3.1 Photo of multimedia journalist. Istock photo by Getty Images.

Jobs in journalism have changed dramatically since the dawn of the Internet in the 1990s. The number of newspaper jobs are down nearly 60 percent from nearly 500,000 in 1990 to 183,000 in 2016, according to the U.S. Bureau of Labor Statistics.[1] Positions in periodicals and books have also dropped, but not by as much as newspapers. Meanwhile, jobs in Internet publishing and broadcasting shot up from just 30,000 in 1990 to nearly 200,000 in 2016.

In broadcast, the number of jobs has remained about the same since 2004, at about 29,000, according to Pew Research Center,[2] but the job titles and descriptions have changed quite a bit.

In today's fast-paced world where consumers can get news any time, any place and just about any kind of device, newsrooms are seeking journalists who truly embrace the concept of being digital first.

Journalism observer and scholar Jeff Jarvis defines digital first as the concept of resetting the "journalistic relationship with the community, making the news organization less a producer and more an open platform for the public to share what it knows. It is to that process that the journalist adds value. She may do so in many forms – reporting, curating, people and their information, providing applications and tools, gathering data, organizing effort, educating participants . . . and writing articles."[3]

Journalists who understand that their content must inhabit the digital space are being hired across platforms – journalists who know how to leverage social media for reporting, disseminating, and promoting stories. Newsrooms are also seeking to hire people who are able to tell stories across platforms and know how to leverage social media to engage the audience and build trust with the community.

Almost every journalist is expected to be "deft at social media reporting via Facebook, Twitter and others," as described in a July 2018 job posting for Journalist written by the Baltimore Sun Media Group.[4]

And an increasing number of journalists – regardless of the medium – being hired in today's market are expected to know how to write under deadline pressure, create online content and shoot and edit video and photos. Indeed, many are being hired specifically as **Multimedia Journalist** (MMJ) or **Multiskilled Journalists** (MSJ). Nexstar, considered one of the largest TV operators in the country, sought an MMJ who "produces, reports, shoots, writes, voices, edits and feeds news production content for all platforms" in summer 2018.[5]

KGW 8 in Portland sought a **Weather Reporter/Multi-Skilled Journalist (MSJ)** who can create "unique and shareable stories for all platforms through memorable writing, photography and editing."[6] In March 2019, Univision sought an MMJ to serve as a "one-person band that will complete a story from onset to end. Must be able to work alone with the camera, to write and edit his/her story, and to interact with the viewers throughout the Univision web page and social media."[7]

In spring 2018, The Tribune Media Company sought an MMJ who could "shoot, edit, write and produce news stories, cover breaking news, establish relationships with the community, produce content for Twitter, Facebook and other social media platforms, and appear on camera on these platforms."[8]

Reporters, producers, and other storytellers are also being hired to serve as **Digital Storyteller** at Gannett, **All Media Journalist** at Cox Media Group, and Morning **Digital Reporter** to "maximize www.lsj.com's peak audience times to drive increased page views" at the *Lansing State Journal*, which is part of the *USA Today* network.[9]

In March 2018, *Bloomberg* in San Francisco posted a job for **Social Velocity Reporter**. The person with this title would be expected "make split-second decisions and understand the tools, trends, platforms and processes behind the most modern strategies for telling stories via social media."[10]

NewsDay Media Group sought a **Social Media Video Producer** "who lives and breathes social media 24/7"[11] in March 2018. That same month, NBCUniversal sought a Digital Content Producer "proficient in social media and SEO [search engine optimization]" for its online E! website.[12]

And WMBF News in Myrtle Beach, South Carolina, in the spring of 2018, posted a job ad seeking an experienced digital journalist who "speaks the social media language, is an Instagram fanatic, Snapchats like a pro, and of course knows how to engage and build an audience on Facebook and Twitter."[13]

Kaiser Health News, a nonprofit news service focused on health care, sought a **Digital Reporter** in early 2018, hoping to find the next Nate Silver of health care.[14] Nate Silver is a well-known journalist who developed a system of forecasting major league baseball player performance and predicted the winner of the 2008 presidential election in 49 of the 50 states. His FiveThirtyEight blog, which was licensed by *The New York Times* for several years, was sold to ESPN in 2013, and Silver is now its Editor in Chief.

Even journalists not trained in social media are finding themselves required to get up to speed and engage via social media. The *ESPN* news team, for example, collaborates with the SportsCenter social team to implement "takeovers" on SportsCenter's social media platforms.[15]

"Inevitably, reporters get more access and better content from athletes and others. It's a natural extension of their credibility and visibility on TV," senior coordinating producer Tim McHugh said. "Simply put, it just makes the content more compelling and memorable, the athletes are often more at ease and engaged with reporters they know or recognize."[16]

Most importantly, newsrooms view people who produce great stories and share and promote their work via social media as part of the editorial staff.

Social media writer Laura Lake defines this new breed of reporters as **Social Media Reporters**, people who "supplement traditional news reporting by adding informative content in media conduits such as blogs, microblogs (such as Twitter), websites, web pages, and other platforms connected with the online community."[17]

Because "social media has become such an important part of the fabric of our culture and society," journalists need to know how to "sift through, analyze, understand and interpret what is going on,"[18] writes Cordelia Hebblethwaite on The Social Media Reporter website, which shows journalists how to organize feeds, locate visuals, verify information, find sources, monitor what's trending, and more.

Beyond Traditional Roles in a Newsroom

Journalists who have developed an expertise in running successful social media campaigns, and driving traffic back to the news site through the power of **Search Engine Optimization** (SEO), are finding new titles and duties that go beyond the traditional role of reporter, producer, and editor.

SEO, briefly stated, is the "process website owners use to help search engines find, index, and rank their web pages, hopefully above competitors' websites. While there are several search engines you can rank on, including Bing and Yahoo, the majority of Internet search (80 percent) is done through Google."[19] (See Chapter 11 How to Measure Success.)

In April 2018, NPR, *Newsweek*, and *The New Republic* were all seeking to hire social media editors. In its listing, *Newsweek* sought a "sharp, motivated, creative, analytical **Social Media Editor** to manage and grow our social footprint across the web."[20] That same month, the *Indianapolis Star* placed an ad for a **Content Coach**, a team leader who could lead coverage in Hamilton County – and create an effective social media strategy to build and engage the audience.[21]

Also, in 2018, *The New Republic* sought an editor who was a "genuine newshound—determined by how many breaking-news notifications you subscribe to—and a disciplined social media writer who understands the potential hazards in distributing bite-sized news at a high speed." This editor, the ad continued, "is responsible for scheduling posts, drafting snappy and effective copy, and tracking key analytics on a consistent basis. The candidate must be a strategic thinker who uses real-time analytics and trending conversations."[22]

NPR sought a Social Media Editor to help "guide the social strategy for NPR for each of its social platforms and evaluates the engagement and performance with the NPR audience."[23]

Politico, a nonpartisan political news site, sought a Digital Editor with "excellent news judgment and multi-tasking abilities who can anticipate news developments, edit breaking stories in a relentless news cycle and curate a dynamic homepage for a die-hard political audience."[24]

In April 2018, WGBH News radio station in Boston posted a job listing for and experienced **Audience Engagement Editor**, "to manage our social media accounts across a number of programs, lead the implementation of our social media strategy and broaden the reach and impact of our radio, television and written stories."[25]

The responsibilities of the audience engagement editor, according to the job post, included: growing the station's social media audience on

Facebook, Twitter, Instagram, and Snapchat, producing social content, including video, images, GIFs, and emerging platform content such as 360 video or live streams, and executing engagement and audience development initiatives, ranging from hashtag campaigns, social ad campaigns, Twitter chats, Reddit AMAs, Facebook Live interviews, and facilitating social media "takeovers."

Education

While many young people are digital natives who are quite comfortable with technology and social media, today's journalist must learn to use social and digital media in a responsible manner that protects his or her professional brand.

To help prepare students and others who want to land or transition into social media journalism, a growing number of journalism schools and centers have incorporated an increasing number of social media classes into their programs and/or classes, and a few have created full-scale social media programs.

- Poynter News University[26] offers a wide variety of online and in-person workshops and courses to help journalists at all levels learn how to use social media for journalism. Courses in April included "Podcasting for Everyone," "Creating an Audience-Focused, Digital First News Organization," and "Social Media Visuals: Tips and Free Tools."
- The Craig Newmark Graduate School of Journalism at CUNY offers a master's degree in Social Journalism. As described on its website, the Social Journalism degree is all about finding new ways to serve communities. It is a master's degree focused on the skills that are hot in journalism today, like engagement, social video, audience growth, social newsgathering and verification, data, analytics, social media tools, design thinking, product development, and more.
- At the University of Florida's College of Journalism and Communications, students can enroll in a 38-unit master's program that will give students a "deep understanding of how to engage audiences through creative content and impactful messaging."[27]
- The University of Southern California (USC) offers a master of Social Digital Media, which "teaches you leadership and management of social media, digital media, and online communities," and allows students to "develop expertise in the practice, theory, and strategies that are essential for success in today's business and social landscape."[28]
- San Francisco State University offers a class called Social Media Journalism, which teaches students how to effectively build their brand across social media platforms.

"Community engagement has a promotional value but it's not about promotion," according to Steve Buttry, director of student media at Louisiana State University's Manship School of Mass Communication. "It's about doing better journalism."[29]

New Job Reality

In the old days, people who helped a newsroom gain more viewers, listeners, or readers were considered part of promotion or marketing teams. Nowadays, journalists at every level of the newsroom experience are expected to help the newsroom attract and engage with its target audience.

In addition, journalists who take the extra time to learn new skills in SEO, advertising, social media, and so on are finding even more jobs that help the newsroom to stand out in an increasingly competitive market.

The bottom line is that news outlets seeking to become digital first are hiring people that can help them leverage technology, the web, and social media to reach and engage their target audience.

Katherine Viner of Britain's *The Guardian*, which launch its digital-first strategy in 2011,[30] added: "Digital is not about putting up your story on the web. It's about a fundamental redrawing of journalists' relationship with our audience, how we think about our readers, our perception of our role in society, our status."[31]

One example of engaging the audience, Viner noted, is when *The Guardian* asked its audience in August 2010 to send them ideas for how to cover the oil spill in the Gulf of Mexico. "We created a Google Doc for readers to post their suggestions, and before we knew it we had ideas from professional divers, marine engineers, physicists, biochemists, mechanical engineers, petrochemical and mining workers, pipework experts. We curated some of the best and subjected them to scrutiny. It was an incredibly rich and deep piece of work, made possible because of the people formerly known as the audience."[32]

Online Comments

Another way that the news media originally sought to engage the public was by opening up comments to their online stories. The problem, however, was that some of these comments turned into personal attacks on the journalists and people featured in the stories. This has now led to many major media outlets, including NPR, CNN, *Popular Science*, and *Scientific American*, cutting off comments to the general public.

In his December 2015 piece for *The Globe and Mail*, writer Russell Smith lamented the decision of CBC and *Toronto Star* in Canada to follow the trend of American publications to "shut off their comments sections – following studies that showed that readers were unconsciously influenced in their judgments of scientific research if they read highly negative comments about it. In other words, comments create bias." Smith wrote:

Has one of the great promises of the Internet finally shown to be false? . . . The democracy that instant free publishing promised, the sense that everyone would have a say – are we bored with this already? It has been fewer than 10 years since comments sections on news stories began to be heavily plugged as avenues for "engagement" and debate, and now many major media outlets are reconsidering their existence.[33]

Even though many media outlets have restricted online comments,[34] many of these same companies allow the public to weigh in through their social media accounts. This, they believe, is a better way of creating the "open platform" that Jarvis described is necessary to be a truly digital first company.

Journalist Michael Skoler, a former Nieman Fellow and former vice president of interactive for Public Radio International, however, says that many of these social media accounts don't allow for true dialogue or engagement with the community.[35]

In his 2009 article for *Nieman Reports*, Skolar wrote:

The truth is the Internet didn't steal the audience. We lost it . . . Today fewer people are systematically reading our papers and tuning into our news programs for a simple reason—many people don't feel we serve them anymore. We are, literally, out of touch. Today, people expect to share information, not be fed it. . . . And they want connection—they give their trust to those they engage with—people who talk with them, listen and maintain a relationship.[36]

Skoler's argument that journalists need to create relationships with their audience and to gain more trust is timely – given the fact that the public's trust in the news media hit an all-time low in 2016.[37]

As consumers are given a multitude of choices of where, when, and how they want to receive their news, journalists and newsrooms must do more within their digital and social platforms to rebuild public trust – and engage the audience in meaningful conversations.

"People aren't fooled by false interaction if they see that news staff don't read the comments or citizen reports, respond and pursue the best ideas and knowledge of the audience to improve their own reporting," Jarvis wrote. "Journalists can't make reporting more relevant to the public until we stop assuming that we know what people want and start listening to the audience."[38]

To create "authentic" dialogue, most media outlets are hiring journalists who are savvy and excited about engaging through social media, something that some newer media companies such as the *Huffington Post*, Politico, and Buzzfeed have been doing for years.

Discussion Questions

1 Do you think your current journalism courses are preparing you to excel at the kind of skills you will need in the news business? Why or why not?
2 What other courses or workshops can you take to learn new skills?
3 Do you think your social media skills will help you get a job in journalism? Explain why or why not.

Exercises

1 Conduct an online search of jobs, using the keyword "journalism," and list the responsibilities for at least three of those positions. Write a short summary on your findings.
2 Look up journalism jobs with "digital" in their titles. What do you think it means to be a digital journalist?
3 Find three dream jobs. What skills would you need to get them? Please list and create a plan of action on how to obtain the skills and education you'll need to get that job.

Notes

1 Bureau of Labor Statistics, "Employment trends in newspaper publishing and other media, 1990–2016," June 2, 2016, https://www.bls.gov/opub/ted/2016/employment-trends-in-newspaper-publishing-and-other-media-1990-2016.htm, accessed April 9, 2018.
2 "Local TV news fact sheet," Pew Research Center, July 12, 2018, http://www.journalism.org/fact-sheet/local-tv-news/, accessed July 15, 2018.
3 Jeff Jarvis, "Digital first: what it means for journalists," *The Guardian*, June 26, 2011, https://www.theguardian.com/media/2011/jun/26/digital-first-what-means-journalism, accessed March 1, 2018.
4 Journalist job posting, Google Jobs, https://www.google.com/search?ibp=htl;jobs&hl=en-US&kgs=e459ab820e7942c7&q=journalism+jobs&shndl=-1&source=sh/x/im/textlists/detail&entrypoint=sh/x/im/textlists/detail#fpstate=tldetail&htidocid=khd8WpKxNurDZ7JuAAAAAA%3D%3D&htiq=journalism+jobs&htivrt=jobs, accessed July 18, 2018.
5 https://www.ziprecruiter.com/c/Nexstar-Media-Group/Job/Reporter,-MultiMedia-Journalist-1-of-2/-in-Waco,TX?ojob=46569cae8492b1e404e70aba007a1dfd, accessed March 25, 2019.
6 Tegna job listing, https://www.jobs.net/jobs/tegna/en-us/job/United-States/Weather-Reporter-MSJ/J3M59H69DWPYC098Y7V/, accessed March 25, 2019.

7 ZipRecruiterjob posting March 2019 https://www.ziprecruiter.com/c/ Univision-Communications,-Inc/Job/Multimedia-Journalist/-in-San-Jose,CA? ojob=8872227e67db6d190d320ded2b8a6ea9, accessed March 25, 2019.

8 Tribune Media Company job posting for Multimedia Journalist, Indeed.com, https://www.indeed.com/jobs?q=Social%20Media%20Journalist&l&vjk=f200 1336867a2508, accessed April 12, 2018.

9 The Job Network, https://jobs.thejobnetwork.com/Job/42643620/online-reporter-job-in-lansing-mi-us, accessed March 25, 2019.

10 Google Jobs, https://www.google.com/search?q=social+media+reporter&rciv =fjb&ibp=htl;jobs&hl=en&gl=US#fpstate=tldetail&htidocid=LCbI5A7pGhkj sYJWAAAAAA%3D%3D&htivrt=jobs, accessed April 11, 2018.

11 *NewsDay* job ad: https://newsday.wd1.myworkdayjobs.com/Newsda/job/ Melville-Pinelawn-Rd/Social-Media-Video-Producer_R360

12 Digital jobs search, Google, https://goo.gl/pSvJqj, accessed March 6, 2018.

13 Lensa job posting, https://lensa.com/digital-content-producer-jobs/myrtle-beach/jd/00c4288eaa6165c77dc95dcd3abeae82, accessed March 25, 2019.

14 Digital Reporter, Kaiser Health News, Google, https://goo.gl/RNBMCd, accessed on April 12, 2018.

15 Molly Mita, "Social Media Reporters Find Success with SportsCenter Social Channel Takeovers," ESPNFrontrow.com, March 6, 2017, last accessed August 11, 2017.

16 Ibid.

17 Laura Lake, "Understanding the Role of a Social Media Reporter," *The Balance*, February 4, 2018, https://www.thebalance.com/understanding-the-role-of-a-social-media-reporter-2295200, accessed April 12, 2018.

18 Cordelia Hebblethwaite, *The Social Media Reporter*, https://medium.com/the-social-media-reporter, last accessed August 11, 2017.

19 Randy Duermyer, "Search Engine Optimization Tutorial," Balance Small Business, April 8, 2018, https://www.thebalancesmb.com/search-engine-optimization-tutorial-1794804, accessed August 3, 2018.

20 Journalismjobs.com, https://www.journalismjobs.com/1643960-social-media-editor-newsweek, accessed April 9, 2018.

21 Journalism.job.com, https://www.journalismjobs.com/1644374-content-coach-gannett-co-incusa-today-network, accessed April 9, 2018.

22 Original job posting no longer available.

23 Entertainmentcareers.net https://www.entertainmentcareers.net/npr/social-media-editor-digital-news/job/257205/?utm_campaign=google_jobs_ apply&utm_source=google_jobs_apply&utm_medium=organic, accessed April 10, 2018.

24 LinkedIn job posting, https://www.linkedin.com/jobs/view/digital-editor-at-politico-957169750/, accessed March 25, 2019.

25 ZipRecruiter, https://www.ziprecruiter.com/c/WGBH/Job/Audience-Engage ment-Editor/-in-Boston,MA, accessed March 25, 2019.

26 Poynter News University, https://www.newsu.org, accessed April 12, 2018.

27 University of Florida http://onlinemasters.jou.ufl.edu/social-media/, accessed on August 31, 2018.

28 Menachem Wecker, "Avoid Social Media MBAs, some students say," USNews. com, March 1, 2012, https://www.usnews.com/education/best-graduate-schools/ top-business-schools/articles/2012/03/01/avoid-social-media-mbas-some-students-say, last accessed August 31, 2018.

29 Elia Powers, "The Rise of the Engagement Editor and What that Means," Mediashift, August 19, 2015, http://mediashift.org/2015/08/the-rise-of-the-engagement-editor-and-what-it-means/, last accessed on August 31, 2018.

30 Dan Sabbagh, "Guardian and Observer to adopt 'digital-first' strategy," *The Guardian*, June 16, 2011, https://www.theguardian.com/media/2011/jun/16/guardian-observer-digital-first-strategy?intcmp=239, accessed March 1, 2018.

31 Katharine Viner, "The rise of the reader: Journalism in the age of the open web," *The Guardian*, October 9, 2013, https://www.theguardian.com/commentisfree/2013/oct/09/the-rise-of-the-reader-katharine-viner-an-smith-lecture, accessed March 1, 2018.

32 Ibid.

33 Russell Smith, "Say bye to the online comments section as you know it," *The Globe and Mail*, December 22, 2015, https://www.theglobeandmail.com/arts/books-and-media/russell-smith-say-bye-to-the-online-comment-section-as-you-know-it/article27906890/, accessed March 1, 2018.

34 Daniel Lee, "NPR, CNN, Other News Sites Hit the Mute Button on Readers," The Federalist.com, July 26, 2017, http://thefederalist.com/2017/07/26/npr-cnn-news-sites-hit-mute-button-readers/, accessed on August 31, 2018.

35 David Squires, "Social Media's Impact on Journalism: How Journalism has morphed into a new type of journalism with the use of social media," *The Social Construction of Media*, October 21, 2016, http://scalar.usc.edu/works/cultures-of-social-media/table-of-contents?path=index, accessed February 28, 2018.

36 Ibid.

37 Jim Norman, "Americans' confidence in institutions stays low," Gallup, June 13 2016, http://news.gallup.com/poll/192581/americans-confidence-institutions-stays-low.aspx, accessed February 28, 2018.

38 Jeff Jarvis, "Digital first: what it means for journalists," *The Guardian*, June 26, 2011, https://www.theguardian.com/media/2011/jun/26/digital-first-what-means-journalism, accessed March 1, 2018.

4 Legal and Ethical Considerations of Using Social Media in Journalism

Figure 4.1 Photo of the words social media written on rolled-up newspaper. Istock photo by Getty Images.

Much attention has been focused on fake news produced by non-journalists, but the truth is that some members of the public are questioning news produced the mainstream media as well. More than three in four Americans polled by Monmouth University Institute in March 2018 said they "believe that traditional major TV and newspaper media outlets report 'fake news,' including 31 percent who believe this happens regularly and 46 percent who say it happens occasionally."[1]

"These findings are troubling, no matter how you define 'fake news.' Confidence in an independent fourth estate is a cornerstone of a healthy democracy," according to Patrick Murray, director of the independent Monmouth University Polling Institute. "Ours appears to be headed for the intensive care unit."[2]

The good news is that a poll released in August 2018 found that more people are trusting TV news. Video Advertising Bureau reported in late 2018 that "news consumers across all ages, ethnicities, income levels, genders, and political affiliation perceive television as an exponentially more trustworthy information platform at all stages of political campaigns."[3]

"As some platforms unintentionally allow the dissemination of unverified news stories and political ads, television is trusted because it provides an environment that features 100 percent professionally produced news," *Forbes* reported.[4]

But the reality is this: journalists face a dual challenge. As they seek to rebuild public trust, journalists must produce groundbreaking, accurate, and informative news stories – and build their identities, create a following, and promote their work and organization through social media.

So, how can journalists do both jobs well?

First Amendment

The First Amendment of the U.S. Constitution states that "Congress shall make no law respecting an establishment of religion or prohibiting the free exercise thereof; or abridging the freedom of speech, or of the press; or the right of the people peaceably to assemble, and to petition the Government for a redress of grievances."[5]

This amendment has protected journalists in the U.S. from government control, but it does not protect those journalists who knowingly print or air stories that are inaccurate and hurt the reputation of others.

Libel is defined as false and defamatory attack in written form on a person's reputation or character. **Slander** is defined as false and defamatory attack in oral form.

For journalists, the greatest defense against libel or slander is truth.

The New York Times v. Sullivan case in 1964 set the precedent by establishing that public figures and public officials must prove that the news outlet in a **libel or slander case** acted in reckless disregard for the truth.

Actual malice means you published something knowing it was false or carelessly published information without checking whether it was true or false.[6]

The standard is different, however, for public figures and public officials. If journalists act in reckless disregard of the truth, they can be found by a judge or jury to have libeled a public figure or officials.

Public figures are defined as:

- People whose achievements or notoriety places them in the public eye.
- People who seek attention by voluntarily thrusting themselves into a public controversy.

NOTE: If they are brought into the public spotlight involuntarily, they may not be public figures.

Public officials are defined as:

- Elected officials and candidates.
- Appointed officials may or may not be public officials. Criteria: Do they have the authority to set policy in the government and are they under public scrutiny to have easy access to the media?

When it comes to private citizens, the burden to show proof is on the journalist or news organization.

> To support a claim for defamation, in most states a private figure need only show negligence by the publisher, a much lower standard than "actual malice." Some states, however, impose a higher standard on private figures, especially if the statement concerns a matter of public importance. You should review your state's specific law in the State Law: Defamation section of the Digital Media Law Project's legal guide for more information.[7]

It's important to note that simply retweeting or posting someone else's content might not get you into legal trouble. Section 230 of the Communications Decency Act protects most websites, including news outlets, from defamation liability for content that's created by a third party.[8]

"Section 230 is as important as the First Amendment to protecting free speech online, certainly here in the U.S.," Emma Llanso, a free expression advocate at the Center for Democracy and Technology, said in a March 2018 NPR article.[9]

Ethical Considerations

The Society of Professional Journalists (SPJ) created a Code of Ethics[10] many years ago, and it continues to be followed by the majority of journalists to this day. The entire SPJ Code of Ethics can be summed into four basic principles:

1   Seek truth and report it.
2   Minimize harm.
3   Act independently.
4   Be accountable and transparent.

The Radio Television Digital News Association (RTDNA) "does not dictate what journalists should do in every ethical predicament; rather it offers resources to help journalists make better ethical decisions – on and off the job – for themselves and for the communities they serve."[11]

And just like the SPJ Code of Ethics, the RTDNA code places truth above all else. "The facts *should* get in the way of a good story. Journalism requires more than merely reporting remarks, claims or comments. Journalism verifies, provides relevant context, tells the rest of the story and acknowledges the absence of important additional information."[12]

There are many other codes for journalists across platforms to follow, but the important thing to remember is that in today's world of 24–7 news, journalists must apply these guidelines to their behavior on social media.

Indeed, most media outlets and journalism schools have added social media to their guidelines on how journalists and journalism students should conduct themselves. For example, the Walter Cronkite School of Journalism and Mass Communication at Arizona State University advises its students to abide by the SPJ Code of Ethics when posting on social media.[13]

NPR, among the most respected radio news stations in the country, updated its Ethics Handbook in 2017 to address some of the ethical dilemmas being faced by many journalists. Its updated policy stated:

> In 2012, when the Handbook was published and the special section was created, the rewards and risks associated with social media were called "new and unfamiliar" . . . Five years later, NPR journalists are active on social media and those rewards and risks aren't new or unfamiliar any more. In fact, one unpleasant aspect has become all too familiar: While NPR journalists generally enjoy their interactions with the public on social media, they have also been the targets of abuse on Twitter and other platforms. We've added new guidance on how to handle such situations.[14]

Among NPR's key rules are the following:

1   Conduct yourself online as you would in any other public circumstances as an NPR journalist.
2   Avoid actions that might discredit your professional impartiality.
3   Don't "shout in all caps" when angry.
4   Don't "take the bait from trolls and sink to their level."
5   Be transparent. Tell readers and listeners what has and hasn't been confirmed.

NPR's updated policy adds that staffers should be mindful that the distinction between private and public social interactions has become less clear.

> Information from a Facebook page, blog entries and tweets — even if they're intended to be personal messages to friends or family — can be easily circulated beyond the intended audiences. The content, therefore, represents us and NPR to the outside world — as do our radio pieces and stories for NPR.org. This applies to the people and organizations we choose to "friend" or "like" online as well. Those are content choices as much as a message or blog post.[15]

Rule of thumb for NPR staffers?

> You should conduct yourself in social media forums with an eye to how your behavior or comments might appear if we were called upon to defend them as being appropriate behavior by a journalist. In other words, don't act any differently online than you would in any other public setting.[16]

NPR, however, does say there is room to be a "little looser with our language on social media. There are words and phrases that, if written with the right tone, are OK. Take 'badass,' for example. Used as a compliment it's a wonderful word."[17]

Other national news outlets have created similar policies regarding social media.

> Dean Baquet, executive editor of *The New York Times*, wrote in a 2017 letter to staff: Social media plays a vital role in our journalism. On social platforms, our reporters and editors can promote their work, provide real-time updates, harvest and curate information, cultivate sources, engage with readers and experiment with new forms of storytelling and voice. We can effectively pull back the curtain and invite readers to witness, and potentially contribute to, our reporting. We can also reach new audiences. But social media presents potential risks for *The Times*. If our journalists are perceived as biased or if they engage in editorializing on social media, that can undercut the credibility of the entire newsroom.[18]

As written in 2017, The *New York Times* guidelines included:

- "Journalists must not express partisan opinions, promote political views, endorse candidates, make offensive comments or do anything else that undercuts *The Times*'s journalistic reputation."
- "Our journalists should be especially mindful of appearing to take sides on issues that *The Times* is seeking to cover objectively."
- "These guidelines apply to everyone in every department of the newsroom, including those not involved in coverage of government and politics."
- "We consider all social media activity by our journalists to come under this policy. While you may think that your Facebook page, Twitter feed, Instagram, Snapchat or other social media accounts are private zones, separate from your role at *The Times*, in fact everything we post or 'like' online is to some degree public. And everything we do in public is likely to be associated with *The Times*."
- "On that same note, we strongly discourage our journalists from making customer service complaints on social media. While you may believe that you have a legitimate gripe, you'll most likely be given special consideration because of your status as a *Times* reporter or editor."
- "Avoid joining private and 'secret' groups on Facebook and other platforms that may have a partisan orientation. You should also refrain from registering for partisan events on social media. If you are joining these groups for reporting purposes, please take care in what you post."[19]

The Los Angeles Times (*LAT*) also has social media guidelines that apply to all newsroom employees, whether they work in editorial or not. Those guidelines include the following:

- "Assume that your professional life and your personal life merge online regardless of your care in separating them. Don't write or post anything that would embarrass the *LAT* or compromise your ability to do your job."

- "Assume that everything you write or receive on a social media site is public and knowable to everyone with access to a computer."
- "Interview sources by phone or in person, when possible, after collecting information online."
- "Do not engage in political advocacy. Just as political bumper stickers and lawn signs are verboten in the offline world for *LAT* editorial employees, so too are partisan expressions in the online world."
- "Also understand that readers may view your 'participation' in a group as your acceptance of its views; be clear that you're looking for story ideas or simply collecting information. Remember that it may not be clear who initiated the contact."
- "Using social media sites in reporting means that you (and the content you exchange) are subject to their terms of service. This can have legal implications, including, but not limited to, the possibility that your interactions could be subject to a third-party subpoena. Any information might be turned over to law enforcement without your consent."[20]

Ethics for Bloggers

The Code of Ethics for Bloggers, Social Media and Content Creators, based on the Code of Ethics for the Norwegian Press, says:

> The content you create today will more than likely outlast both the content's relevance and your own lifetime and it is of vital importance that it be a truthful representation of the topic at hand not only for those who access it today but for those who access it in the distant future.[21]

Among its chief guidelines is to "tell the truth at all times," never confuse facts with opinion, and disclose your affiliations.[22] The guidelines go on to say:

> To preserve your own trustworthiness and integrity as a Content Creator, always state any relation, financial, personal, political or otherwise, to the subject or topic you are presenting. Bias, even if it is only perceived as such, immediately discredits your account unless you warn of it first. In simple terms; if you have a political affiliation that colors your judgment, say so; if you are employed by or received money from the subject you are covering, say so; if you were given gifts or preferential treatment in return for a positive review or commentary, say so.[23]

Online News Association

The Online News Association (ONA) Social Newsgathering Ethics Code is seeking the support of news outlets around the world to "endorse a set of standards relating to the gathering and use of content created by members of the public." Among its chief rules of this code are that newsrooms, journalists, and others should "endeavor to verify the authenticity of user-generated content."[24]

ONA also acknowledges that:

> social media and blogs are important elements of journalism. They narrow the distance between journalists and the public. They encourage lively, immediate and spirited discussion. They can be vital newsgathering and news-delivery tools. As a journalist you should uphold the same professional and ethical standards of fairness, accuracy, truthfulness, transparency and independence when using social media as you do on air and on all digital news platforms.[25]

ONA adds that social media comments and postings "should meet the same standards of fairness, accuracy and attribution that you apply to your on-air or digital platforms."[26]

Discussion Questions

1   Do you believe that journalists should be bound by a code of ethics when sharing their own views on social media? Why or why not?
2   Do you think news sites should close the comments section? Why or why not?
3   Do you believe it's possible to separate your personal views from your professional ones?
4   Based on what the *Los Angeles Times* says about social media, would you want to work for that news outlet? Why or why not?
5   Based on what the *New York Times* says about secret groups on Facebook, would you want to work there? Why or why not?

Exercises

1   Teamwork: Read through the social media guidelines for NPR, *The New York Times*, the *Los Angeles Times*, and one other media outlet of your choice. Are there any rules your team would change? Please note and explain why they should be changed.
2   Teamwork: Review the social media guidelines from SPJ, ONA, RTDNA, and at least one other organization. Note chief differences among them with your team.
3   Teamwork: Using the ONA "Build Your Own Ethics Code" site, create a social media policy that you believe journalists should follow. Go to this site: https://ethics.journalists.org/

Notes

1 Monmouth University Poll, April 2, 2018, https://www.monmouth.edu/polling-institute/documents/monmouthpoll_us_040218.pdf/, accessed May 30, 2018.
2 Ibid.
3 Tony Silber, "Survey: U.S. Electorate, Burned by Fake News, Trusts TV News More Than Other Sources," *Forbes*, August 6, 2018, https://www.forbes.com/sites/tonysilber/2018/08/06/survey-u-s-electorate-burned-by-fake-news-trusts-tv-news-more-than-other-sources/#212ea27d11ad, accessed March 25, 2019.
4 Tony Silber, "Survey: U.S. Electorate, Burned by Fake News, Trusts TV News More Than Other Sources," *Forbes*, August 6, 2018, https://www.forbes.com/sites/tonysilber/2018/08/06/survey-u-s-electorate-burned-by-fake-news-trusts-tv-news-more-than-other-sources/#212ea27d11ad, accessed August 26, 2018.
5 First Amendment, U.S. Constitution, Legal Information Institute, https://www.law.cornell.edu/constitution/first_amendment, accessed April 15, 2018.
6 Reporters Committee for Freedom of the Press, "Defining actual malice," https://www.rcfp.org/browse-media-law-resources/digital-journalists-legal-guide/defining-actual-malice, accessed July 16, 2018.
7 Digital Media Law Project, http://www.dmlp.org/legal-guide/proving-fault-actual-malice-and-negligence, accessed July 16, 2018.
8 Cornell Law School, 47 U.S. Code 230, https://www.law.cornell.edu/uscode/text/47/230, accessed July 18, 2018.
9 Alina Selyukh, "Section 230: A key legal shield for Facebook, Google is about to change," March 21, 2018, https://www.npr.org/sections/alltechconsidered/2018/03/21/591622450/section-230-a-key-legal-shield-for-facebook-google-is-about-to-change, accessed July 18, 2018.
10 SPJ Code of Ethics, https://www.spj.org/pdf/ethicscode.pdf, accessed April 15, 2018.
11 RTDNA Code of Ethics, https://www.rtdna.org/content/rtdna_code_of_ethics, accessed July 18, 2018.
12 Ibid.
13 "Social Media Guidelines for Student Journalists, Cronkite School, Arizona State University, https://cronkite.asu.edu/degree-programs/admissions/student-resources/social-media-guidelines, accessed July 16, 2018.
14 NPR Ethics Handbook, http://ethics.npr.org/tag/social-media/, accessed July 16, 2018.
15 Ibid.
16 Ibid.
17 Ibid.
18 *The New York Times* social media guidelines, https://www.nytimes.com/2017/10/13/reader-center/social-media-guidelines.html
19 Ibid.
20 *Los Angeles Times* social media guidelines, http://asne.org/resources-ethics-lasocial, accessed July 18, 2018.
21 Morten Rand-Hendriksen, https://mor10.com/code-of-ethics-for-bloggers-social-media-and-content-creators/, accessed July 18, 2018.
22 Ibid.
23 Ibid.
24 ONA Social Newsgathering Ethics Code, https://toolkit.journalists.org/social-newsgathering/, accessed July 18, 2018.
25 Ibid.
26 Ibid.

5   The Rise of Fake News and Its Impact on Journalism

Figure 5.1 The word, FAKE NEWS, made up of chopped up newspaper. Istock photo by Getty Images.

As stated in Chapter 1, the Hutchins Commission called for a truthful, comprehensive account of the day's events and a forum for the exchange of comment and criticism. Now, as agencies of mass communication, major social media platforms such as Facebook are facing perhaps even more scrutiny than the big news media outlets faced 75 years ago.

Though executives of some of these companies refuse to take on the moniker of news providers, the research shows that social networks have become a key channel of communication for news, defined by Kovach and Rosenstiel as the basic purpose of journalism.

"The purpose of journalism is not defined by technology, nor by the journalists or the techniques they employ," Kovach and Rosenstiel claimed in their book *The Elements of Journalism*. "The principles and purposes of journalism are defined by something more basic; the function news plays in the lives of people."[1]

Facebook has two billion active users and a majority of those users get news on the site, according to the Pew Research Center. "Looked at as a portion of all U.S. adults, this translates into just under half (45 percent) of Americans getting news on Facebook."[2] Pew also found that 18 percent of all Americans now get news on YouTube and 11 percent get news on Twitter.[3]

As a result, many major social media platforms have become agencies that facilitate thought and discussion, advance the progress of civilization or thwart it, which is how the Hutchins Commission described major news media outlets.

Of the greatest concern is fake news.

"Fake news is enemy No. 1 right now," reported Molly Wood in the Marketplace blog. "Companies and governments are trying to figure out who should be in charge of spotting misinformation and getting rid of it. MIT researcher Sinan Aral has found that the not-true stuff, what he calls 'false news,' is not only hard to stop, but also really effective."[4]

"There's a story, for example, suggesting that Barack Obama was injured in an explosion," Aral told Marketplace. "That wiped out a $130 billion of equity value in a single day."[5]

Zuckerberg at Capitol Hill Hearings

At an April 2018 hearing on Capitol Hill, lawmakers had questioned Facebook CEO Mark Zuckerberg about the company's failure to protect the public from privacy breaches, hacking, and fake news.

It was the second time that Facebook had been called to Capitol Hill in six months. In fall 2017, executives from Facebook, Twitter, and other social platforms were forced to answer questions about Russia's ability to use those platforms to polarize the American public with incendiary and often untrue ads on everything from police relations and religion to border control, with one account publishing an ad that read, "Satan: If I win, Clinton Wins!"[6]

At the April 2018 hearings, Zuckerberg again apologized to lawmakers for his platform's failure to prevent Russia from hacking into its network during the 2016 presidential election. He also apologized to lawmakers for Cambridge Analytica's improper access to the personal data of 87 million users, which was used to target voters in the 2016 presidential election.[7]

Zuckerberg, however, stopped short of calling his social media company a news media company.

"When people ask us if we're a media company — or a publisher — my understanding of what the heart of what they're really getting at is, 'Do we feel responsibility for the content on our platform?' The answer to that, I think, is clearly yes," Zuckerberg said.[8]

Zuckerberg, however, has acknowledged the powerful role Facebook plays in informing the public by taking steps to remove content deemed false or even offensive.

In August 2018, Facebook, along with Apple, YouTube, Spotify, and other companies, "took down podcasts and channels from U.S. conspiracy theorist Alex Jones, saying . . . that the Infowars author had broken community standards."[9]

Jones is a well-known radio host who runs the popular Infowars website. Facebook told the news media it removed his pages "for glorifying violence, which violates our graphic violence policy, and using dehumanizing language to describe people who are transgender, Muslims and immigrants, which violates our hate speech policies."[10]

In July 2018, just three months before U.S. primary elections, Facebook removed "32 Pages and accounts from Facebook and Instagram because they were involved in coordinated inauthentic behavior. This kind of behavior is not allowed on Facebook because we don't want people or organizations creating networks of accounts to mislead others about who they are, or what they're doing."[11]

Whether Facebook, Twitter, and other networks see themselves as media companies or not, multimedia journalist Alex Janin of NowThis said she believes that it falls on those companies to do more to protect the public.

"They really do have a responsibility to do more . . . in terms of regulations," said Janin, a multimedia journalist who graduated from the University of Southern California with a B.A. in Broadcast and Digital Journalism. "Not sell ads to companies like Cambridge Analytica or allow

Figure 5.2 Headshot of Alex Janin. Photo credit: Michele Janin, Alex's mother.

people to say whatever they want or post whatever they want" is a good start, she added.[12]

At the April 2018 hearings, U.S. Representative Greg Walden, an Oregon Republican, brought up the idea of imposing regulations on Facebook and other social media giants through legislation. "I think it is time to ask whether Facebook may have moved too fast and broken too many things."[13]

Senator Bill Nelson, a Florida Democrat, added: "If Facebook and other online companies will not or cannot fix these privacy invasions, then we will."[14]

Fake news and data theft were not the only problems facing Facebook in recent years. The ability to broadcast live on social media, initially perceived as a technological breakthrough, erupted in controversy after dozens of people streamed suicides, rapes, and other violent acts. In one case, a 12-year-old girl streamed her suicide – and after two weeks of complaints, Facebook took it down.[15]

And, just as many newsrooms ultimately did after the release of the Hutchins Commission's findings, Facebook has taken steps to self-regulate its business, including measures to reward those who report data abuse, making ad and ad pages more transparent, including source information on news stories, and taking steps to restrict data access.[16]

Even before the Capitol Hill hearings, Facebook began taking steps to address public concerns about fake and inaccurate news and information on the platform. It also gave a nod to the work of journalists and others who seek truth, transparency, and accountability.

"When it comes to advertising on Facebook, people should be able to tell who the advertiser is and see the ads they're running, especially for political ads," said Ron Goldman, Vice President of ads at Facebook, in an October 2017 press release. "That level of transparency is good for democracy and it's good for the electoral process. Transparency helps everyone, especially political watchdog groups and reporters, keep advertisers accountable for who they say they are and what they say to different groups."[17]

In her blog post, Lyons said that the company is removing accounts and content that violate their policies, reducing the distribution of false news and the incentives to create it, and giving users more context on the stories they see. Facebook has taken other steps to fight fake news. "False news is a money maker for spammers and a weapon of state actors and agitators around the world," said product manager Tessa Lyons, adding: "Misinformation is bad for our community and bad for our business."[18]

Twitter

Twitter, considered the most popular social network among journalists,[19] has been grappling with fake news for years. Indeed, a comprehensive MIT study of every major contested news story in English tweeted by three million users for ten years found that false rumors and fake news reached more people and spread much faster than accurate stories. "Falsehood diffused significantly farther, faster, deeper, and more broadly than the truth in all categories of information, and the effects were more pronounced for false political news than for false news about terrorism, natural disasters, science, urban legends, or financial information," the authors of the MIT study wrote. "We found that false news was more novel than true news, which suggests that people were more likely to share novel information. Whereas false stories inspired fear, disgust, and surprise in replies, true stories inspired anticipation, sadness, joy, and trust."[20]

In January 2018, Twitter revealed that more than 50,000 Russia-linked accounts used its service to post automated material about the 2016 presidential election.[21] Understanding the power and influence of its network, Twitter executives also have taken steps to regulate its platform.

In February 2018, disinformation ran rampant on Twitter during the high school shooting in Parkland, Florida, that killed 17 students. A fake account attributed to Bill O'Reilly (former talk show host on Fox News) claimed that there were two shooters, and/or that the shooter was a comedian. Other tweets falsely accused other people of being the shooter.[22]

And in April 2018, disinformation ran rampant after a woman opened fired at the YouTube headquarters in San Bruno, California, injuring three people before killing herself. Some of the most popular tweets were being written by people inside YouTube, but as it turns out, not all of those tweets were accurate or even real.

Vadim Lavrusik, a product manager at YouTube, tweeted: "Active shooter at YouTube HQ. Heard shots and saw people running while at my desk. Now barricaded inside a room with coworkers."[23]

Lavrusik's tweet in itself should be considered a great example of **citizen journalism**, which essentially acknowledges the growing phenomenon of citizens taking an active role in the collection, production, and dissemination of news. Indeed, his earlier tweets were among the first bits of information that informed the public about the shooting.

The problem, however, was that someone hacked Lavrusik's account and tweeted: "PLEASE HELP ME FIND MY FRIEND I LOST HIM IN THE SHOOTING" – linking to a photo of YouTube video creator Daniel "Keemstar" Keem. There was no indication that Keem was at the scene, according to *Business Insider*.

Twitter has sought to refine its tools and improve the speed of its response to false tweets, hoaxes, and hacking. "In light of the horrific attack at YouTube headquarters this week, we're sharing more detail on how we're tackling an especially difficult and volatile challenge: our response to people who are deliberately manipulating the conversation on Twitter in the immediate aftermath of tragedies like this," said Del Harvey, Twitter's vice president of Trust and Safety.[24]

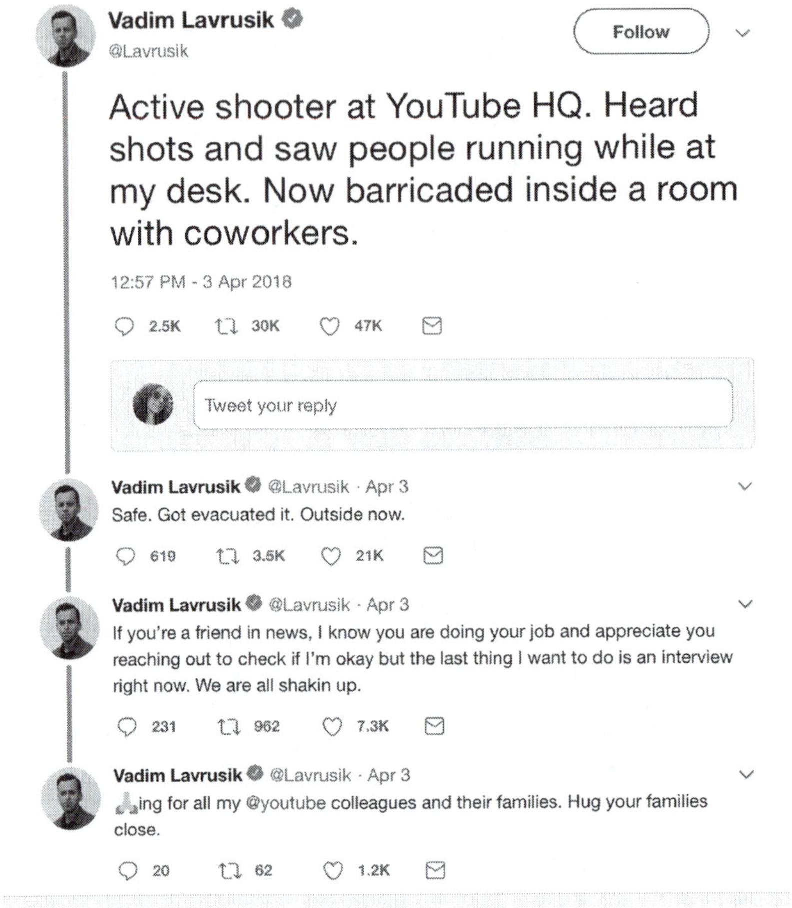
Vadim Lavrusik
@Lavrusik
Follow
Active shooter at YouTube HQ. Heard shots and saw people running while at my desk. Now barricaded inside a room with coworkers.
12:57 PM - 3 Apr 2018
2.5K 30K 47K
Tweet your reply
Vadim Lavrusik @Lavrusik · Apr 3
Safe. Got evacuated it. Outside now.
619 3.5K 21K
Vadim Lavrusik @Lavrusik · Apr 3
If you're a friend in news, I know you are doing your job and appreciate you reaching out to check if I'm okay but the last thing I want to do is an interview right now. We are all shakin up.
231 962 7.3K
Vadim Lavrusik @Lavrusik · Apr 3
ing for all my @youtube colleagues and their families. Hug your families close.
20 62 1.2K

Figure 5.3 Vadim Lavrusik's tweets. Twitter.

"People come to Twitter first to learn about news and events unfolding in real-time, and we're committed to ensuring that the information they receive is credible and authentic," Harvey explained in a company blog post.[25]

> Whether it's real-time rescue efforts of Hurricane Harvey survivors in Texas, capacity-building with Indian NGOs [non-government organizations] who aid flooded communities, verifying credible voices after major events, or sending prompts to French citizens in the wake of the November 2015 terrorist attacks in Paris, our goal is to provide support to people in times of crisis, and show people what matters most.[26]

YouTube

With close to two billion users, YouTube also has come under fire for spreading fake news. In February 2018, a video suggesting that a student at Marjory Stoneman Douglas High School in Florida was an actor paid to speak out during the Florida shooting became YouTube's No. 1 trending video.

YouTube ultimately removed the video and its executives acknowledged that the video should never have appeared in its Trending section. YouTube also took steps to clamp down on fake channels making money from advertising after it was revealed that ads were appearing next to extremist content.[27]

Google

Google, which owns YouTube, has also taken steps to fight fake news, changing its algorithm to "surface more authoritative content."[28]

Donald J. Trump @realDonaldTrump
Follow

Google search results for "Trump News" shows only the viewing/reporting of Fake News Media. In other words, they have it RIGGED, for me & others, so that almost all stories & news is BAD. Fake CNN is prominent. Republican/Conservative & Fair Media is shut out. Illegal? 96% of....

8:02 AM - 28 Aug 2018

26,439 Retweets 93,420 Likes

33K   26K   93K

Donald J. Trump @realDonaldTrump · Aug 28
....results on "Trump News" are from National Left-Wing Media, very dangerous. Google & others are suppressing voices of Conservatives and hiding information and news that is good. They are controlling what we can & cannot see. This is a very serious situation-will be addressed!

27K   20K   73K

Figure 5.4 Donald Trump's tweet on Google and fake news. Twitter.

"Today, in a world where tens of thousands of pages are coming online every minute of every day, there are new ways that people try to game the system," Ben Gomes, Google's Vice President of engineering, wrote in an April 2017 company blog. "The most high-profile of these issues is the phenomenon of 'fake news,' where content on the web has contributed to the spread of blatantly misleading, low quality, offensive or downright false information."[29]

In August 2018, the White House alleged that Google "systematically discriminates against conservatives on social media and other platforms."[30] Google has denied those allegations.

"When users type queries into the Google Search bar, our goal is to make sure they receive the most relevant answers in a matter of seconds," a Google spokesperson said. "Search is not used to set a political agenda and we don't bias our results toward any political ideology."[31]

Snapchat

In November 2017, Snapchat responded to concerns over fake news on its platform by separating chats and stories from friends on the left and stories from publishers, creators, and others on the right.

"Until now, social media has always mixed photos and videos from your friends with content from publishers and creators," Snapchat announced in its November 2017 press release. "While blurring the lines between professional content creators and your friends has been an interesting Internet experiment, it has also produced some strange side-effects (like fake news) and made us feel like we have to perform for our friends rather than just express ourselves."[32]

Meanwhile, researchers at the University of Michigan recently developed an algorithm that "identifies telltale linguistic cues in fake news stories could provide news aggregator and social media sites like Google News with a new weapon in the fight against misinformation."[33]

The Echo Chamber Effect

An **echo chamber** is defined by *Techopedia* as a "situation where certain ideas, beliefs or data points are reinforced through repetition of a closed system that does not allow for the free movement of alternative or competing ideas or concepts. In an echo chamber, there is the implication that certain ideas or outcomes win out because of an inherent unfairness in how input is gathered."[34]

Despite the efforts of social network executives to fight fake news, most scholars agree that newsfeeds on most social platforms serve as echo chambers of information and disinformation. That's because the algorithms used by social networks determine what people see on their newsfeeds based on what they *want* to see. Therefore, if someone likes and shares stories from Infowars.com, for example, they will continue to see stories from that site – despite the fact that some say the site contains numerous inaccurate, misleading, and fake news stories.

In the new world order, a person gets to decide what they want to see. Under the Uses and Gratification Theory, this makes sense. No longer does the mass audience have to wait for a particular TV network or newspaper to tell them what the big stories of the day area. This can be good for some, but truly bad for a society that uses this information to weigh in on issues and even vote.

Role of Bloggers and Citizen Journalists

Beyond powerful algorithms, individuals have a huge role to play in the creation or proliferation of fake news. Journalists, however, are not the only ones reporting breaking news. **Citizen journalists** are becoming a

Figure 5.5 Headshot of Owen Thomas. Courtesy of Liz Hafalia of *SF Chronicle*.

force to be reckoned with. Indeed, some individuals have gained quite the following.

While many welcome the addition of more voices, critics say people with no training or education in journalism may not understand the ethical and legal values that have guided American journalists for decades.

This is one reason why trained journalists play such a critical role in today's fast-changing media landscape, says *San Francisco Chronicle* Business Editor Owen Thomas.

"Social media is never going to match the professional journalist on the scene," says Thomas, who supervises The *Chronicle*'s business and technology coverage. "What we found in citizen journalism is . . . there's a lot of citizen but not much journalism. The consistency is not there. It's hit or miss."[35]

Thomas, the former editor-in-chief of *ReadWrite*, a technology news site, also worked as managing editor of *Valleywag*, a popular blog billed as a "tech gossip rag" about Silicon Valley personalities that ran from 2006 to 2015, also believes that the public should be more skeptical of everything they read, see and hear online.

"Video editing and manipulation that uses artificial intelligence that creates very realistic images . . . for example, face swapping," Thomas explained. "The software can swap one politician's face for another and create a video where it looks like someone else is speaking. So, all of these technological developments have made me far less optimistic about mass-distributed, citizen-captured video and far more convinced of the value to journalists who are committed to professional objectivity . . . because you may not be able to trust the video out there. That was something I didn't think about a couple years ago."[36]

Case in point is the story of Eric Tucker. On November 9, 2016, Tucker posted photos of buses on his Facebook and Twitter accounts, telling his friends and followers that he was convinced that anti-Trump protesters were arriving in buses to Austin, Texas. Within hours, Trump's biggest community on Reddit, "The Donald," shared Tucker's unconfirmed hunch as fact.

The Reddit post was then picked up by numerous conservative groups, and even some news outlets. A Fox News story cited Tucker's tweet, writing "observers online are claiming that, in some cases, protesters were bused to the scenes – a telltale sign of coordination."[37]

By the time it was all over, Tucker's tweet was shared at least 16,000 times on Twitter and more than 350,000 times on Facebook.[38] It was even shared in a tweet by President Trump.

While most social media users would love a tweet or post to get this much attention, the problem was Tucker's report about protesters in buses was false.

Tucker apologized in his November 12, 2016 blog post. "As I have said before, I value the truth," Tucker wrote. "I will remove the Tweet so more people can have a higher proportion of truth in their lives. I also want us all to refrain from repeating information that is likely untrue so that we can

Eric Tucker
@erictucker

Follow ⌄

And BOOM! The old big bad post is gone!
Its memory shall live on! Thanks all! Let's
keep the conversation moving!
blog.erictucker.com/2016/11/11/why ...

9:57 PM - 11 Nov 2016

Figure 5.6 Tucker's tweet. Twitter.

have greater credibility when our evidence is stronger." He added: "I am
not a professional blogger nor a professional journalist. I do hope to find
more ways to make a difference. Being involved in political discourse is vital
to democracy."[39]

Tucker's tweet is an example of how social media has the power to turn one person's tweet – fake or real – into a major news story, noted the authors of "Audiences' acts of authentication in the age of fake news: A conceptual framework," published in September 2017 in the *New Media & Society Journal*. "Unintentional fake news, satirical pieces, and news that is purposely fake have become part of our daily news diet," the authors wrote. "Deliberately false news items have done everything, from amusing us to confusing us. In a more sinister vein, they have also served to facilitate improperly founded political mobilization."[40]

Fake News to Some May Not Be Fake News to All

While those trained in journalism may know what constitutes fake news, not everyone agrees on what constitutes fake news.

"The way some people, including some politicians, use the term fake news is . . . anything you disagree with or anything you find uncomfortable," says Thomas of *The San Francisco Chronicle*. "There's fake news, fake audio, fake video, fake documents. In the thoroughly digital world we live in, we have to be suspicious and skeptical all the time."[41]

Thomas adds that some people think that the stories traditional news outlets are producing are fake. "The converse of that is people are being suspicious of fair reporting. Hard-working journalists trying to do their job and trying to present the facts as best they can. The fake news phenomenon is very much about the real news being called fake and the fake news being mistaken for real. I don't know how you really solve that."[42]

While social media networks and powerful search engines such as Google have taken steps to control the spread of fake news,[43] the popularity of social media and advances in technology have irrevocably changed the way people consume news and information. Kindles, iPads, and smartphones have made it easy for people to tune into what's happening while they're on the go. Very few people wait for the 6 o'clock news or the arrival of their morning paper anymore.

Thus, the power that the traditional news media once held has diminished. Large news outlets and networks are no longer the gatekeepers of the news, as noted in Chapter 1. Nowadays, a citizen such as Eric Tucker has the potential of becoming a powerful town crier. And under the Agenda-Setting Theory, citizens can also set the agenda of what they consider to be most important to the public.

Conclusion

Just as traditional media companies did nearly 75 years ago, many social media networks are confronting public outcry over sensationalism, invasion of privacy, conglomeration, and fake news. And even though many executives from these companies deny they are in the business of news, the fact is this: a growing number of people, especially young people, get their news from search engines, news feeds, mobile alerts, and so on.

As such, traditional media outlets are no longer the gatekeepers of news. While the rise of different voices and perspectives can be seen as good for a democratic society, there are some challenges. Namely, it's become increasingly difficult for the public to ferret out "fake" news.

While most social networks and search engine companies have tried to address these problems, the fact is that the view of traditional newsrooms as gatekeepers of news vital to public discourse has changed dramatically. Nowadays, the audience has the power to decide when they want to receive the news, how to receive it, and from whom. And thanks to highly sophisticated algorithms, the audience often receives news that aligns with their likes, dislikes, and values.

This means that journalists and newsrooms that believe in the importance of truth, accuracy, and balance are having a harder time reaching the mass audience. Part II provides journalists with concrete steps to practice social media journalism – everything from how to verify the information they now rely on via social media to how to stand out in a crowded field and inform the public.

Discussion Questions

1   Are traditional news outlets still the gatekeepers of news? Why or why not?
2   Do you think Facebook is a gatekeeper of news? Why or why not?
3   Do you think Google has done enough to prevent or curb fake news? Why or why not?
4   Do you think it's the responsibility of social networks and search engines to prevent fake news from showing up in your newsfeed or searches? Why or why not?

Exercises

1   Review the Hutchins Commission report with a partner or team. Which comments apply to social networks of today?
2   Review the Bloggers Code of Ethics. Which guidelines seem similar to those in the SPJ Code of Ethics? Please list them and explain why they are similar.

Notes

1 Bill Kovach and Tom Rosenstiel. *The Elements of Journalism: What Newspeople Should Know and the Public Should Expect.* Updated and revised 2007.

2 Jeffrey Gottfried and Elisa Shearer, News Use Across Social Media Platforms 2017, Pew Research Center, September 7, 2017, http://www.journalism. org/2017/09/07/news-use-across-social-media-platforms-2017/, accessed April 13, 2018.

3 Ibid.

4 Molly Wood, *Marketplace*, August 27, 2018, https://www.marketplace.org/ 2018/08/24/tech/one-problem-fake-news-it-really-really-works, accessed August 31, 2018.

5 Ibid.

6 Cecilia Kang, Nicholas Fandos, and Mike Isaac, "Russia-financed ad linked Clinton and Satan," *The New York Times*, November 1, 2017, https://www. nytimes.com/2017/11/01/us/politics/facebook-google-twitter-russian-inter ference-hearings.html, accessed April 15, 2018.

7 Brian Barrett, "How to Check if Cambridge Analytica Could Access Your Facebook Data," *Wired*, April 9, 2018, https://www.wired.com/story/did-cam bridge-analytica-access-your-facebook-data/, accessed April 15, 2018.

8 Alina Selyukh, "Facebook Founder And CEO Mark Zuckerberg Testifies On Capitol Hill," April 10, 2018, WJCT Public Media, https://news.wjct.org/ post/facebook-founder-and-ceo-mark-zuckerberg-testifies-capitol-hill, accessed March 26, 2019.

9 Rich McKay, "Apple, YouTuber and others drop conspiracy theorist Alex Jones," Reuters, August 6, 2018, https://www.reuters.com/article/us-apple-infowars/ apple-youtube-and-others-drop-conspiracy-theorist-alex-jones-idUSKBN 1KR0MZ, accessed August 31, 2018.

10 Ibid.

11 Facebook Newsroom, https://newsroom.fb.com/news/2018/07/removing-bad-actors-on-facebook/#what-weve-found.

12 Author's interview with Alex Janin, April 2018.

13 Tony Romm, "Mark Zuckerberg survived 10 hours of questioning by Congress, but will the U.S. now move to regulate Facebook?" National Post, April 12, 2018, https://nationalpost.com/news/world/facebooks-zuckerberg-survived-10-hours-of-questioning-by-congress-but-will-lawmakers-now-move-to-regu late-the-social-network, accessed March 26, 2019.

14 Craig Timberg, Tony Romm, and Elizabeth Dwoskin, "Zuckerberg apolo-gizes, promises reform as senators grill him over Facebook's failings," *The Washington Post*, April 10, 2018, https://www.washingtonpost.com/business/ technology/2018/04/10/b72c09e8-3d03-11e8-974f-aacd97698cef_story. html?utm_term=.48c1b6069ea5, accessed April 13, 2018.

15 Kristine Phillips, "A 12-year-old girl live-streamed her suicide. It took two weeks for Facebook to take the video down," January 15, 2017, *The Washington Post*, https://www.washingtonpost.com/news/the-intersect/wp/2017/01/15/a-12-year-old-girl-live-streamed-her-suicide-it-took-two-weeks-for-facebook-to-take-the-video-down/?utm_term=.940cff68e7d1, accessed on January 6, 2018.

16 Facebook Newsroom, https://newsroom.fb.com/news/2018/, accessed April 15, 2018.

17 Rob Goldman, Vice President of Ads, "Update on Our Advertising Transparency and Authenticity Efforts," October 27, 2017, https://newsroom.fb.com/

news/2017/10/update-on-our-advertising-transparency-and-authenticity-efforts/, accessed April 15, 2018.

18 Facebook Newsroom, https://newsroom.fb.com/news/2018/06/hard-ques tions-fact-checking/

19 Rebecca Lerner, "Twitter tops Snapchat – Among Journalists, at Least," Forbes. com, May 26, 2017, https://www.forbes.com/sites/rebeccalerner/2017/05/26/ twitter-tops-snapchat-among-journalists-at-least/#458ad7367b79, accessed April 15, 2018.

20 Soroush Vosoughi, Deb Roy, and Sinan Aral, "The Spread of True and False News Online," *Science*, March 9, 2018, http://science.sciencemag.org/con tent/359/6380/1146, accessed April 17, 2018.

21 John Swaine, "Twitter admits far more Russian bots posted on election than it had disclosed," *The Guardian*, January 19, 2018, https://www.theguardian.com/ technology/2018/jan/19/twitter-admits-far-more-russian-bots-posted-on-election-than-it-had-disclosed, accessed April 15, 2018.

22 Nicole Lee, "Twitter's fake news problem is getting worse," engadgetl.com, February 18, 2018, https://www.engadget.com/2018/02/17/twitter-s-fake-news-problem-is-getting-worse/, accessed April 15, 2018.

23 Rob Price, "Someone Hacked a YouTube Employee's Twitter Account to Spread Misinformation About the Shooting," *Business Insider*, http://www. businessinsider.com/youtube-employee-twitter-hacked-spread-hoax-office-shooting-2018-4, accessed July 20, 2018.

24 Del Harvey, "Serving the public conversation during breaking events," Twitter company blog, April 5, 2018, https://blog.twitter.com/official/en_us/topics/ company/2018/Serving-the-Public-Conversation-During-Breaking-Events. html, accessed July 23, 2018.

25 Ibid.

26 Ibid.

27 Stuart Lauchlan, "YouTube clamps down on 'fake news' channels cashing in," April 10, 2017, https://diginomica.com/2017/04/10/youtube-clamps-fake-news-channels-cashing/, accessed July 20, 2018.

28 Daisuke Wakabayashi, "As Google Fights Fake News, Voices on the Margins Raise Alarm," The New York Times, September 26, 2017, https://www. nytimes.com/2017/09/26/technology/google-search-bias-claims.html, accessed February 1, 2018.

29 Ben Gomes, "Our latest improvements for Search," Google company blog, April 25, 2017, https://blog.google/products/search/our-latest-quality-improvements-search/, accessed July 20, 2018.

30 Tony Romm, "Trump's economic adviser: 'We're taking a look' at whether Google searches should be regulated," *The Washington Post*, August 28, 2018, https://www.washingtonpost.com/news/morning-mix/wp/2018/08/28/ trump-wakes-up-googles-himself-and-doesnt-like-what-he-sees-illegal/?utm_ term=.831391a3d5b0&wpisrc=nl_most&wpmm=1, accessed August 31, 2018.

31 Andrew Griffin, "Trump news: google finally responds after president launches attack on search giant," August 2018, https://www.independent.co.uk/life-style/ gadgets-and-tech/news/trump-news-google-response-us-president-algorithm-results-statement-a8511531.html, accessed September 4, 2018.

32 Snapchat press release, November 29, 2017, https://www.snap.com/en-US/ news/post/introducing-the-new-snapchat/, accessed April 16, 2018.

33 *Michigan News*, "Fake news detector algorithm works better than a human," August 21, 2018, https://news.umich.edu/fake-news-detector-algorithm-works-better-than-a-human/.

34 Definition of echo chamber, https://www.techopedia.com/definition/23423/ echo-chamber, accessed July 20, 2018.

35 Author's interview with Owen Thomas in spring 2018.

36 Ibid.

37 Asher Price, "How an Austin tweet about Trump protests became a national conspiracy," *American-Statesman*, November 11, 2016, https://www.mystatesman. com/news/state--regional-govt--politics/how-austin-tweet-about-trump-pro tests-became-national-conspiracy/vTBkvkxbtEq6zougOw0TDL/, accessed May 24, 2018.

38 Sapna Maheshwari, "How fake news goes viral: a case study," *The New York Times*, Nov. 20, 2016, https://www.nytimes.com/2016/11/20/business/media/how-fake-news-spreads.html, accessed May 24, 2018.

39 Eric Tucker, "Why I'm removing the 'Fake Protests' Twitter post," Hope for an Intelligent Future blog, https://blog.erictucker.com/2016/11/11/why-im-con sidering-to-remove-the-fake-protests-twitter-post/, accessed May 24, 2018.

40 Edson C Tandoc, Jr, Richard Ling, Oscar Westlund, Andrew Duffy, Debbie Goh, and Lim Zheng Wei, "Audiences' acts of authentication in the age of fake news: A conceptual framework," *New Media & Society Journal*, September 21, 2017, https://doi-org.jpllnet.sfsu.edu/10.1177/1461444817731756, accessed May 11, 2018.

41 Author's interview with Owen Thomas, spring 2018.

42 Ibid.

43 Chaim Gartenberg, "Google News Initiative announced to fight fake news and support journalism," *The Verge*, March 20, 2018, https://www.theverge.com/2018/3/20/17142788/google-news-initiative-fake-news-journalist-subscriptions, accessed May 24, 2018.

Part II

The Practice of Social Media Journalism

6 Personal Branding for Journalists

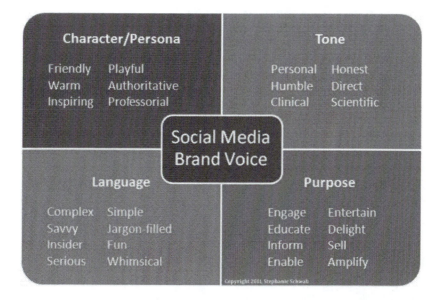

Figure 6.1 Social Media Brand Voice

In a March 2014 article for *Vanity Fair,* James Wolcott accurately captured the struggle of today's journalist: "In our own millennial time, novelists and reporters excelling in expressionistic flourishings are depreciated in favor of those who provide snapshot analysis, crunchy sound bites, and political handicapping—expertise that has an obvious social utility with a personable face attached."[1]

While Wolcott expresses a frustration shared by many journalists, the truth is print and broadcast journalists and authors have been marketing themselves for years.

"Exploiting your unique personality to get ahead professionally is as old as Dale Carnegie's How to Win Friends and Influence People," wrote Ann Friedman in a 2015 *The New Republic* article.[2]

The big difference today is *how* we market ourselves.

In the old days, journalists built up their reputation by writing a front-page story in a major newspaper or producing a top TV news story seen by upwards of millions of people.

These days, however, the road to fame, rather recognition, is much harder. That's because the audience no longer goes to one particular news site or broadcast program for all their news and information. Indeed, many find news on social media and/or search engines. And many more set up alerts for the kind of news they want to receive.

That is why an increasing number of newsrooms have hired marketing teams skilled in social media to promote their stories on social networks.[3]

The reality, however, is that promotion at the organizational level through social media company and business pages is not enough. The public wants to get to know the journalists behind the stories.

Professors Avery E. Holton and Logan Molyneux wrote in "Identity lost? The personal impact of brand journalism," that developing a relationship with the audience is also part of the "value proposition individual journalists make to their employers, both present and future: I can bring you this information, this writing expertise, and also this group of followers who are already interested in my content."[4] A great way for journalists to develop a relationship with the audience is by developing their own **personal brand**.

A personal brand, a term coined by motivational speaker and author Tom Peters in 1997,[5] is defined as who you are, what you stand for, and how others perceive you. The personal brand is made up of your bio, your profile, your photos, your activities, your causes, your stories, and even your tweets and social posts. In other words, your personal brand is pretty much everything you do or say – both online and offline.[6]

It's important to present yourself in a way that best reflects your personality, values, and principles as a journalist. Remember what Amazon's Jeff Bezos said? "Your brand is what others say about you when you leave the room."[7]

How Do You Build an Authentic Brand?

Most journalists hate marketing themselves, but building a strong personal brand is less about self-promotion and more about sharing stories with the widest audience possible.

"Journalists' work eventually ends up in front of an audience, and journalists are beginning to realize the necessity of branding themselves for their audience, especially using social media," Holton and Molyneux wrote in their article on branding in journalism.[8]

For journalists looking for new gigs or jobs, a strong personal brand is key. In 2017, 70 percent of employers use social media to screen job candidates before hiring them, up from 11 percent in 2006.[9]

CareerBuilder also found that 54 percent of employers decided not to hire a candidate based on their social media profile, half of employers said they checked current employees' social media profiles, and more than a third reprimanded or fired an employee for inappropriate content.[10] The survey also found that nearly 60 percent of employers said they were less likely to interview a candidate they can't find online.[11]

It's a "win-win situation" for reporters all around the world, says Lizzie Jespersen in her article on personal branding in the UK. "The benefit to a journalist's career is notable."[12]

Jespersen added that a "reporter's social media presence has become increasingly important to potential employers, because it allows them to understand that reporter's voice and gives them a sneak peek into how the reporter would engage with readers."[13]

According to Holton and Molyneux, many newsrooms require journalists to create and maintain social media accounts that promote their stories, and some companies require employees to make changes to their profiles and bios.

> While reporters noted freedom in individual branding early on, they overwhelmingly saw it shifting to an organizational function wherein they were asked to make changes, some subtle and some significant, to the ways in which they presented themselves and their content on social media platforms.[14]

Those changes, the authors added, include adding organization names and logos, providing fewer links to outside stories, and engaging with the organization through hashtag conversations.[15]

Three questions to answer BEFORE you build your personal brand

There are three questions you'll want to answer in formulating your own personal brand:

1   Who is your audience?
2   What do you do best?
3   What is your **unique promise of value**?

Personal branding strategist Shahab Anari says people who know their "unique promise of value – what differentiates them from other professionals – will find it easier to elevate themselves on social media, as they will know exactly who they are targeting and therefore develop a stronger fan base."[16]

But before you tackle your unique promise of value, let's answer the first question:

1   Who is your audience?

As an aspiring journalist, you'll need to decide who you serve – or rather, who you want as your audience. The audience could be people in your age range, at your school, or both. Your audience could be national or restricted to the West Coast of the United States.

Many students may believe that they are not ready to pinpoint their job or even a place to work, but it's important to set a course to reach your goals. Think about your dream job. Where do you see yourself in five years? Jot down your five top choices. Note how they are different or the same. Are they all large news outlets? Are your dream jobs in television or radio? Do you see yourself at *Vogue*, NPR, or *National Geographic*? Who are your role models? Do you envision yourself as an Anderson Cooper of CNN or Lesley Stahl of *60 Minutes*?

Once you decide on the kind of journalist you want to be or the type of organization you want to work for, think about *their* audience. What are the demographics? Are they older? Highly educated? Do they come from a certain area in the country, or are they international? By learning about the audience of your dream job or publication, you will have a better understanding of who you will serve.

Once you know who you want to serve, the next question to answer is what do you do best? Do you have a product or service to provide? If your service is writing stories that inform the public, decide how you do it best. If you know you write well about sports, that is one of your gifts. It's probably difficult to write about all sports well, so name the teams or sports you enjoy covering the most. To figure this out, you'll want to answer the second question:

2   What do you do best?

To answer this question, think about the things you have loved to do since your earliest memory. If you enjoy hiking, biking, and other outdoor activities, you might consider pursuing a career as an environmental journalist, covering global warming, climate change, and other issues that our public should know about.

If you've always loved sports but stopped playing because of an injury or change in interest, you might be the perfect person to cover the Golden State Warriors or the Dallas Cowboys. If you find yourself following every story about the president and the White House, you'd make a great political correspondent.

Of course, there are many journalists who serve as utility players, meaning they cover a wide range of issues – so that is also a talent, and something you might consider as well.

The other thing you'll want to think about is how you share these stories. Are you a videographer? Do you love the written word the most? Or do you prefer to listen to podcasts and perhaps even produce your own podcast? Well then, let recruiters know that you have a talent in one or all of these areas. Admittedly, most networks and news outlets are looking for multimedia journalists (MMJs), which means journalists who can do it all, as discussed in Chapter 3.

When recruiters are assessing your abilities, they will also want to know how long you've been doing the kind of work you say you're good at, and where you've done this work. Be sure to list the number of years you've written for your high school or college publication.

Once you decide what you do best, you must decide how you do it uniquely. To figure out what makes you unique, you'll want to answer the final question:

3   What is your unique promise of value? In other words, how do you do it different from everyone else?

Recruiters want to know what makes you stand out from thousands of other talented college students vying for that one producing or reporting internship at NBC Bay Area or the *Los Angeles Times*. For example, if you do a weekly podcast on hip hop, how or why is it different from the hundreds of other podcasts on hip hop?

Perhaps your podcast is unique because you bring in comedians as guests, or you offer a first-person view as a young woman on sports. Or maybe you shoot with a camera that uses new technologies such as 360-degree video, or include interactivity when telling stories, allowing viewers to choose which section of the story to view next?

Personal Brand Statement

So, now that you have answered all three questions, you're ready to draft your **personal brand statement**.

Think about the personal brand statement as your elevator pitch. If an editor at *The New York Times*, for example, asks why they should hire you, what would you say? Imagine a personal brand statement being like a succinct cover letter that can be shared online and across social networks.

Even though you now know your target audience, what it is you do best, and your unique promise of value, you'll need to also consider something else for social media – and that would be your **character attributes**.

According to Stephanie Schwab of Social Media Explorer, a social media brand voice should include persona or character, tone, language, and purpose.[17] For example, if you want to work at Buzzfeed, notice that the website has a playful persona, a personal tone, fun language, and its purpose seems to lean toward delight and entertainment.

However, if you want to work at *National Geographic*, their persona appears to be authoritative, their tone is scientific, language is complex, and purpose seems to be about educating the public.

Meanwhile, NPR is quite professional in persona, direct in tone, serious in language, and its purpose seems to be about informing the public.

Once you settle upon your attributes, you'll want to craft your personal brand statement. Here is one example of a personal brand statement written for a student journalist:

It's all about the headline. It's about getting your point across in the most direct way you can. These personal statements are very good example of this, in just a few lines I have to get my message of why I want do a degree in Journalism across to my prospective universities. That is one of the reasons why I love to write, the challenge of putting over a complex thought or concept to a large audience of people and convey it in such a way everybody will understand it. As the great writer Hemingway once said, "My aim is to put down on paper what I see and what I feel in the best and simplest way."[18]

Your personal brand statement can now be used as your script when crafting your bio for Twitter, your profile for LinkedIn, and bios for all other social media accounts that you use. Just remember, you'll want to consider all aspects of a social media profile, which are spelled out here.

Username

In either case, it's important to start by creating a username that reflects your values as a journalist. For example, if you're a tech writer, it might be fun to call yourself TechYumi. If you're a sports writer, you might choose SportswithYumi as a username. Also, try to be consistent across platforms so you can be discovered easily.

Profile Photos

The first thing that people see is your photo. So, if you want them to respond to you as a journalist who aims to be fair and impartial, you'll want to choose a photo that exhibits these qualities. For LinkedIn, for example, it's best to choose a photo that is focused on your shoulder level and above.

Bio

The bio is an important piece of real estate on each platform because it's often the reason that sources and potential subjects of your story or news package will reach out to you, or more importantly get back to you when you call or text them. You can craft your bio by using elements of your personal brand statement, as outlined here.

Class Activities

1   Jot down three newsrooms or journalists you admire or want to be like.
2   Research the audience for each of these outlets or journalists and note at least two similarities and two differences.

3   Describe the demographics of each newsroom or journalist.
Using Figure 6.1, explain how your persona, tone, language, and purpose will match at least one of your three dream jobs.
4   Break into pairs and interview your partner for about ten minutes about what they do best, how they do it uniquely, and who they serve.
5   Ask to check out your partner's bios on social media, LinkedIn profile, blogs, and other sites. Once each person is done with the interview, please write the personal brand statement for your partner (not you).

Should You Get Verified?

Notice any differences between these two Facebook pages?

Both accounts can be found via a quick search on Facebook, but only one of these pages is verified. Notice the circle with a checkmark next to former U.S. President Barack Obama's name? That is the page that Facebook has deemed authentic.

Figure 6.2 Screenshot of Facebook page for Barack Obama U.S.A. Facebook.

Figure 6.3 Screenshot of Facebook page for Barack Obama U.S.A. with checkmark. Facebook.

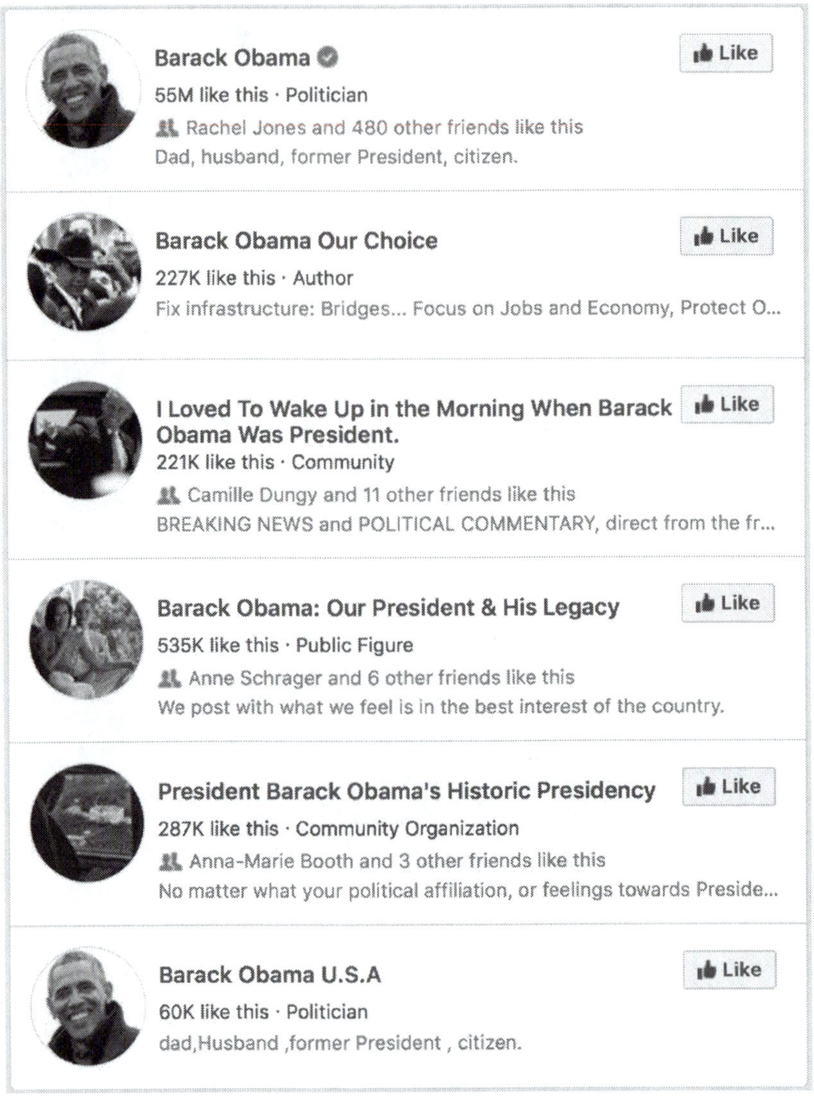

Barack Obama ✓   👍 Like
55M like this · Politician
👥 Rachel Jones and 480 other friends like this
Dad, husband, former President, citizen.

Barack Obama Our Choice   👍 Like
227K like this · Author
Fix infrastructure: Bridges... Focus on Jobs and Economy, Protect O...

I Loved To Wake Up in the Morning When Barack   👍 Like
Obama Was President.
221K like this · Community
👥 Camille Dungy and 11 other friends like this
BREAKING NEWS and POLITICAL COMMENTARY, direct from the fr...

Barack Obama: Our President & His Legacy   👍 Like
535K like this · Public Figure
👥 Anne Schrager and 6 other friends like this
We post with what we feel is in the best interest of the country.

President Barack Obama's Historic Presidency   👍 Like
287K like this · Community Organization
👥 Anna-Marie Booth and 3 other friends like this
No matter what your political affiliation, or feelings towards Preside...

Barack Obama U.S.A   👍 Like
60K like this · Politician
dad,Husband ,former President , citizen.

Figure 6.4 Screenshot of just some of the search results for Barack Obama on Facebook. Facebook.

This is an important distinction in an era where just about anyone can create an account and pretend to be someone else.

"Fact is, anyone can create a page and put anyone's name to it with no accountability, writes brand consultant Will Burns. "Which doesn't matter much when social media is about cat videos and pictures of kids – or even fake teenage 'Finsta' accounts. But when another country uses it to divide us it matters a lot."[19]

Burns was referring to the discovery that companies linked to Russia had created fake accounts during the 2016 U.S. presidential election to spread likes and misinformation about some of the candidates. Though Facebook ultimately removed these accounts, many more continue to spring up, not just on Facebook but on many other social platforms.

That is why Burns believes the process of setting up pages or accounts needs to change. "Some form of identity verification in social media would guarantee that every account is linked to a registered user," Burns said. "Call it a license or a permit or whatever. But each user must register with a real name, a real address, be issued an account number and perhaps a secret code. Not unlike the security surrounding credit cards today. Without it, you can't open a Facebook or Twitter or Instagram or YouTube account."[20]

One way that Facebook and some other social networks are trying to help the public understand the authenticity of an account is to verify certain businesses and brands by giving them a verification badge.

Twitter

Twitter has verified countless celebrities, politicians and brands, but in late 2017, it paused its verification program. While CEO Jack Dorsey says his "intention is to open verification to everyone,"[21] the reality is that to date, the company has only verified big names.

Facebook

In her May 2018 article, marketing professional Kristen Lodge explains how to get verified on social media.[22] To get verified on Facebook, she said, you must:

- Comply with Facebook's terms of service.
- Include a cover photo, profile photo, acceptable page name, and content.
- Enable the Follow feature.
- Provide a photo ID.
- Explain why you should be verified.
- Include relevant URLs to prove people are interested in your content.

Another option is for brands to get the gray verification badge, which is easier to obtain.

To get this gray checkmark, you'll need a publicly listed phone number or business document (such as a phone bill) to start the verification process.

Figure 6.5 Screenshot of Society of Professional Journalists Facebook page with gray verification badge. Facebook

Instagram

Instagram just introduced a trio of new features to make the network a "generally safer and more authentic place to hang out." In late August, the company made the process of applying for verification much more straightforward. "While it's too early to tell if Instagram will be handing out more verified badges to users, they've at least made the process much more transparent," according to TechCrunch. "Now, any user can request to be verified with a few steps."[23]

Pinterest

Pinterest offers a verification badge to celebrities, brands, or the news media. "The goal of this checkmark," Pinterest says on its website, "is to help people to find the accounts they're looking for (for example, you should be able to easily distinguish Abraham Lincoln's Pinterest account from the Pinterest account for an Abraham Lincoln fan site.)"

LinkedIn

There is currently no verification badge on LinkedIn.

Conclusion

"Those who have mastered Twitter, Facebook and other sites, however, have significantly elevated their professional profiles," Denise-Marie Ordway wrote in an article for the Harvard Kennedy School Shorenstein Center. "Some journalists have amassed giant followings. For example, CNN anchor Anderson Cooper has nearly 10 million Twitter followers. *New York Times* columnist Nicholas Kristof has 2.2 million."[24]

Before you come up with your usernames and bios, think about your goals as an aspiring journalist. Understand that your social and online presence will be how most recruiters find and judge you. Create a personal brand statement and align your branding across platforms.

Discussion Questions

1 Do you think journalists in the old days promoted themselves? Why or why not? Offer three examples.
2 Is personal branding expensive? Please explain.
3 What can students hoping to break into journalism do to build a strong personal brand?

Exercises

1 Using the personal attributes chart in Figure 6.1, define your personal attributes.
2 Imagine that you have to start a new blog. What would you name it? Explain.
3 Find three examples of young people in journalism who have created a strong personal brand. Explain why.
4 Find three examples of journalists who have not done enough to create and promote their personal brand. Explain why.

Notes

1 James Wolcott, "From Ink to Inc. Big-name literary branding isn't new – look at Twain or Hemingway. But today, even novice writers must nurture a social-media presence. Arianna Huffington, Nate Silver, and Ezra Klein have branded their way to the top of Journalism 2.0," *Vanity Fair*, April 2014, https://www.vanityfair.com/culture/2014/04/journalism-brands-social-media, accessed September 4, 2018.
2 Ann Friedman, "Me, Inc." The New Republic, September 28, 2015 https://newrepublic.com/article/122910/my-paradoxical-quest-build-personal-brand, accessed March 26, 2019.
3 Avery E. Holton and Logan Molyneux, "Identity Lost: The Personal Impact of Brand Journalism," *Journalism*, Vol. 18, Issue 2, pp. 195–210. Article first published online November 3, 2015, https://doi-org.jpllnet.sfsu.edu/10.1177/1464884915608816, accessed July 18, 2018.
4 Ibid.
5 Matt Arnerich, "What's next for personal branding?" Personal Branding Blog, May 21, 2018, https://goo.gl/4aUdbj, accessed June 10, 2018.
6 Undercover Recruiter, https://theundercoverrecruiter.com/how-craft-your-personal-brand-statement/, accessed June 14, 2018.

7 Startupvitamins.com, http://startupquotes.startupvitamins.com/post/77385350314/your-brand-is-what-other-people-say-about-you, accessed July 18, 2018.

8 Avery E. Holton and Logan Molyneux, "Identity Lost: The Personal Impact of Brand Journalism," *Journalism*, Vol. 18, Issue 2, pp. 195–210. Article first published online November 3, 2015, https://doi-org.jpllnet.sfsu.edu/10.1177/1464884915608816, accessed July 18, 2018.

9 Cision PR Newswire, "Number of employers using social media to screen candidates at all-time high, finds latest CareerBuilder study," June 15, 2017, https://www.prnewswire.com/news-releases/number-of-employers-using-social-media-to-screen-candidates-at-all-time-high-finds-latest-careerbuilder-study-300474228.html, accessed June 14, 2018.

10 Ibid.

11 Ibid.

12 Ibid.

13 Ibid.

14 Avery E. Holton and Logan Molyneux, "Identity Lost: The Personal Impact of Brand Journalism," *Journalism*, Vol. 18, Issue 2, pp. 195–210. Article first published online November 3, 2015, https://doi-org.jpllnet.sfsu.edu/10.1177/1464884915608816, accessed June 10, 2018.

15 Ibid.

16 Ibid.

17 Stephanie Schwab, "Finding your Brand Voice," March 31, 2011, *Social Media Explorer*, https://socialmediaexplorer.com/content-sections/tools-and-tips/finding-your-brand-voice/, accessed November 7, 2018.

18 Journalism personal statement, Studential.com, https://www.studential.com/personal-statement-examples/journalism-personal-statement, accessed Nov. 7, 2018.

19 Will Burns, "Is It Time To Require Identity Verification For Everyone Using Social Media?," Forbes, Feb. 22, 2018, https://www.forbes.com/sites/willburns/2018/02/22/is-it-time-to-require-identity-verification-for-everyone-using-social-media/#6579fcf78683, Accessed March 27, 2018.

20 Ibid.

21 Hamza Shaban, "Twitter wants to open verification to everyone," *The Washington Post*, March 9, 2018, https://www.washingtonpost.com/news/the-switch/wp/2018/03/09/twitter-says-it-will-open-verification-to-everyone/?utm_term=.040d35929267, accessed September 4, 2018.

22 Jason Murdock, "Twitter Verification: Everyone will soon have a blue tick, CEO Jack Dorsey says," Newsweek, March 9, 2018, https://www.newsweek.com/how-get-verified-twitter-process-be-open-everyone-ceo-jack-dorsey-says-837590, accessed March 27, 2019.

23 Taylor Hatmaker, "You can now apply to get a verified badge on Instagram — here's how," Techcrunch.com, August 28, 2018, https://techcrunch.com/2018/08/28/instagram-how-to-get-verified/, accessed September 4, 2018.

24 Denise-Marie Ordway, "Journalism branding: Impact on reporters' personal identities," Harvard Kennedy School Shorenstein Center, December 19, 2017, https://journalistsresource.org/studies/society/news-media/brand-journalism-impact-reporter-personal-identity, accessed June 1, 2018.

7 How to Tweet Without Getting Fired

Nowadays, most journalists tweet, post, share, comment, and like as part of their jobs. Forty percent of 1,080 U.S. journalists surveyed by Indiana University journalism professors Lars Willnat and David Weaver said social media networks are "very important" to their work and more than a third said they spend between 30 and 60 minutes each day on social networking sites.[1]

The 2017 Global Social Journalism Survey by Cision (a software company aimed at marketing professionals) found that 90 percent of 257 journalists from around the world said they used social media for work at least once a week. Nearly half of those respondents said they "could not successfully complete their work without social media."[2]

The survey also found that 67 percent of the respondents said publishing was a very important function of social media. About 60 percent stated that interacting with their audience was important, and about 46 percent said social media was important for monitoring the news.[3]

There are some key differences between a traditional news story that appears in a newspaper, online news site, or broadcast station. Namely, humor, wit, and other more relaxed characteristics are often welcome by followers, friends, and connections on social media.

Journalists frequently share the lighter side of themselves on social media, and some offer their opinions as well. But how much humor and opinion should journalists offer while staying true to the SPJ Code of Ethics, which include remaining free of the appearance of bias?

"To varying degrees, these practices clash with long-standing ideals such as distance, neutrality, or balanced reporting, and represent one of the many possible alterations of norms and standards around journalism in digital spaces," Svenja Ottovordemgentschenfelde of The London School of Economics and Political Science wrote in study of political journalists' use of Twitter. "Similarly, the unprecedented immediacy of Twitter has amplified the demand for real-time news delivery as well as journalists' hunger to be first in breaking a story, raising concerns around speed over traditional standards such as fact-checking, verification, and accuracy."[4]

Though some people believe there ought to be a separation between what journalists do on company time and their own time, dozens of journalists have learned the hard way that personal tweets are not as personal as you think.

In June 2017, *Breitbart* writer Katie McHugh was fired after tweeting: "There would be no deadly terror attacks in the U.K. if Muslims didn't live there" in the wake of the London Bridge attack that killed eight and injured 48 people.[5]

In May 2017, Denver Post sports columnist Terry Frei was fired after tweeting: "Nothing specifically personal, but I am very uncomfortable with a Japanese driver winning the Indianapolis 500 during Memorial Day weekend."[6] The Denver Post apologized to the public for Frei's "disrespectful and unacceptable tweet," and added that it did not "represent what we believe nor what we stand for."[7]

In June 2017, CNN host Reza Aslan apologized for calling President Trump a "piece of shit" on Twitter, but he was fired by the cable news network about a week later.

In October 2017, ESPN anchor Jemele Hill was suspended for two weeks after weighing into the controversy between NFL players and owners over the right to kneel during the national anthem.

ESPN public Editor Jim Brady, in his column, said Hill was suspended because this and several other tweets calling for action tread "close to activism."

I believe she made a mistake . . . Although she's a commentator, she's also still a journalist. The job of a journalist is to present facts and let consumers

Figure 7.1 Screenshot of Reza Aslan's apology after calling President Trump an expletive. Twitter.

Jemele Hill ✔
@jemelehill

Follow ⌄

If you strongly reject what Jerry Jones said, the key is his advertisers. Don't place the burden squarely on the players.

> **Tiffani** 🌸😀✒️🙏 @SoundCheckMama
>
> Replying to @SoundCheckMama @jemelehill
>
> Write to the advertisers' corporate offices, post on their social media pages, make ourselves heard and seen.

7:50 PM - 8 Oct 2017

💬 1.2K   🔁 4.0K   ♡ 11K   ✉️

Figure 7.2 Screenshot of one of Jemele Hill's tweets that got her suspended by ESPN. Twitter.

ESPN PR ✔
@ESPNPR

Follow ⌄

ESPN's Statement on Jemele Hill:

ESPN'S STATEMENT ON JEMELE HILL

"Jemele Hill has been suspended for two weeks for a second violation of our social media guidelines. She previously acknowledged letting her colleagues and company down with an impulsive tweet. In the aftermath, all employees were reminded of how individual tweets may reflect negatively on ESPN and that such actions would have consequences. Hence this decision."

ESPN

12:19 PM - 9 Oct 2017

💬 4.2K   🔁 2.9K   ♡ 4.3K   ✉️

Figure 7.3 Screenshot of ESPN's PR statement on Jemele Hill. Twitter.

come to their own conclusions, not to skip over that step by resorting to name-calling and inflammatory labels. Whatever one thinks of ESPN's political and election guidelines, she also clearly violated the policy about avoiding political commentaries unless they are related to sports.[8]

In March 2018, Jimmy Pitaro, the new president of ESPN, told *The Washington Post*: "If you ask me is there a false narrative out there, I will tell you ESPN being a political organization is false. I will tell you I have been very, very clear with employees here that it is not our jobs to cover politics, purely."[9]

Hill wrote in her own statement that her departure was of her own choosing.

Jemele Hill ✔
@jemelehill

⬭ Follow ⌄

Over the last several weeks, there have been a lot of rumors about my job status. Today is my last day at ESPN.

More from me on closing one of the most special chapters in my life:

September 14, 2018 at 10:34 AM

When I started at ESPN in 2006, I had no idea that such a wonderful journey would take place over the next 12 years. This was the place where I became the best version of myself, both personally and professionally.

However, the time has come for me to begin a new chapter in my life.

There are so many people to thank, but it's worth me singling out a few that were instrumental during my time at ESPN.

To my friend, brother and former co-h Michael Smith: I love you and you mac me better in every possible way. I'm p of everything we did, because nobody sold tapes out the trunk quite like us.

And to the rest of my ESPN colleague am humbled and forever grateful to h worked with you. I am in awe of your talents. I'll always be rooting for you.

7:40 AM - 14 Sep 2018

💬 4.2K   ⇄ 5.2K   ♡ 37K   ✉

Figure 7.4 Sreenshot of Jemele Hill's statement on leaving ESPN on her Twitter account. Twitter.

Fourth Estate

Why are journalists scrutinized more than the average citizen when it comes to what they say on social media? One big reason is that journalists are part of the **Fourth Estate**, which typically refers to a group other than the usual powers (elected officials, judges, etc.) that wields influence in the politics of a country.[10]

To hold others accountable, journalists must also be held accountable. And that means journalists should be fair, accurate, and willing to hear from all sides of the issue, even if they don't personally agree with someone or something. In other words, journalists should be free – or appear to be free – of bias, as stated in the SPJ Code of Ethics.

But what happens when a journalist shows favor for a particular candidate in a personal tweet or post? Will other politicians still want to talk with her or him?

Probably not.

And that's why an increasing number of newsrooms are making it clear that what journalists say on social media – even during their own time – matters.

Conclusion

From now own on, think about your brand every time you decide to post something to your various accounts. Does the message reflect how you want others to see you? This applies to your responses, your shares, and your likes. The audience views you in terms of everything you do on social media, not just the posts you personally author. If you are working for a news company, find out what their policies are for posting on social media. If you are working for yourself, think about how you want to be viewed as a professional.

As established earlier in this book, journalists must take extra care when engaging with their audience on social media, even when they do it on their own time. That's because the public expects journalists to be free of bias, or the appearance of bias, in their reporting. If journalists have already made up their mind about a certain politician or an important issue, it would be hard for anyone to believe that the journalist was giving all sides of the story.

Group Activity

Question: Should a reporter be fired for tweeting on their own time?

> **Example 1**: Katie Hopkins, a controversial radio presenter and columnist for the London Broadcasting Company, was fired

(continued)

(continued)

after calling for a "final solution" to Islamic terrorism in a tweet. Numerous celebrities and other critics lambasted Hopkins for making what they believe was a direct reference to the extermination of Jewish people by Hitler.

Activity: Research articles on Katie Hopkins to determine what she posted on social media. Try to find the exact tweet. Decide as a group whether you think Hopkins should have been fired and state why or why not.

Example 2: NFL reporter Bart Hubbuch was fired from the *New York Post* in January 2017 for a tweet comparing President Trump's inauguration to the terrorist 9/11 attacks and the Japanese attack on Pearl Harbor.

Activity: Research what Hubbuch said that got him into trouble. Try to find the exact tweet. Decide as a group whether you think Hubbuch should have been fired and state why or why not.

Notes

1 Lars Willnat and David H. Weaver, "The American Journalist in the Digital Age, Findings," School of Journalism, Indiana University, http://archive.news.indiana. edu/releases/iu/2014/05/2013-american-journalist-key-findings.pdf, accessed August 11, 2017.
2 Staff Writer, Business Tech, "How journalists use social media – and the impact of fake news," September 13, 2017, https://businesstech.co.za/news/media/198376/how-journalists-use-social-media-and-the-impact-of-fake-news/, accessed February 28, 2018.
3 Ibid.
4 Svenja Ottovordemgentschenfelde, "Organizational, Professional, Personal: An Exploratory Study of Political Journalists and Their Hybrid Brand on Twitter," *Journalism*, Vol. 18, Issue 1, pp. 64–80. First published onlne July 8, 2016, http://journals.sagepub.com.jpllnet.sfsu.edu/doi/pdf/10.1177/1464884916657524, accessed June 20, 2018.
5 Rosie Gray, "Why Brietbart fired an editor for a tweet," June 7, 2017, https://www.theatlantic.com/politics/archive/2017/06/why-breitbart-fired-an-editor-for-a-tweet/529437/, accessed June 14, 2018.
6 Scott Allen and Cindy Boren, "Denver Post columnist fired after 'disrespectful' tweet about Japanese driver's Indianapolis 500 victory," *The Washington Post*, May 30, 2017, https://www.washingtonpost.com/news/early-lead/wp/2017/05/29/denver-post-sportswriter-issues-apology-after-facing-backlash-for-indy-500-tweet/?noredirect=on&utm_term=.91a231c71cd2, accessed June 14, 2018.
7 *The Denver Post*, May 29, 2017, https://www.denverpost.com/2017/05/29/denver-post-statement-terry-frei/?utm_source=All+Poynter+Subscribers &utm_campaign=8649e19a79-EMAIL_CAMPAIGN_2017_05_30&utm_

medium=email&utm_term=0_5372046825-8649e19a79-257947065, accessed June 14, 2018.

8 Jim Brady, "ESPN navigating uncharted political, social and controversial waters," October 11, 2017, ESPN website, http://www.espn.com/blog/ombudsman/ post/_/id/887/espn-navigating-unchartered-political-social-and-controversial-waters, accessed June 14, 2018.

9 Ben Strauss, "ESPN president wants less politics at network: 'It is not our jobs'," *The Washington Post*, August 17, 2018, https://www.washingtonpost.com/sports/ espn-president-wants-less-politics-at-network-it-is-not-our-jobs-to-cover-pol itics/2018/08/17/6d54c706-a252-11e8-8e87-c869fe70a721_story.html?utm_ term=.a33d0c683aab, accessed September 3, 2018.

10 Dictionary.com, http://www.dictionary.com/browse/fourth-estate, accessed June 14, 2018.

8 How to Find Sources, Stay on Top of Trends, and Verify Information

In the old days, law enforcement officers would alert the public about a shooting or missing person through the news media, sending press releases (announcements sent to the news media), and making phone calls to journalists. Nowadays, their communications strategy involves much more, including social media.

On August 26, 2018, the day that deputies in Jacksonville Sherriff's Office, Florida discovered that there had been a mass shooting at the Jacksonville Landing, they immediately notified the public through Twitter.

For those worried about fake news, this account was verified, which – as stated earlier – means a user will see a small blue circle with a checkmark next to the name of the account. This little blue circle tells users that Twitter has checked out the user and verified they are who they say they are. This is important in today's world, where dozens or hundreds of people might use the name of Lady Gaga or Disney to attract followers.

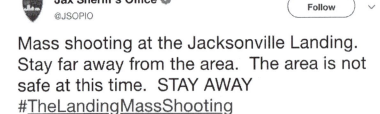

Figure 8.1 Screenshot of 11:13 a.m. tweet from Jacksonville Sheriff's Office during the mass shooting in August 2018. Twitter.

Jax Sheriff's Office ✔
@JSOPIO

(Follow) ∨

There are inaccurate numbers being distributed by local and national media. This is fluid and as soon as we have confirmed numbers they will be released. Please remember this Twitter @JSOPIO is the only official source of information.

> Jax Sheriff's Office ✔ @JSOPIO
> Mass shooting at the Jacksonville Landing. Stay far away from the area. The area is not safe at this time. STAY AWAY #TheLandingMassShooting

2:36 PM - 26 Aug 2018

💬 29   🔁 844   ♡ 1.4K   ✉

Figure 8.2 Screenshot of Jacksonville Sheriff's office 2:36 p.m. tweet saying it's the official account for news on the shooting. Twitter.

In addition, Sheriff's deputies also reminded the public on Twitter that this account was the only one containing official information.

To keep others safe, they continued to tweet updates.

The alerts provided by deputies from the Jacksonville Sheriff's Office informed journalists as well. In some cases, those tweets were included in the actual news story, a trend that is becoming more common among news outlets.

In today's digital-first landscape, journalists have to include social media in their effort to stay on top of breaking news and keep in touch with sources. Luckily, there are hundreds of ways to stay on top of the news for relatively no cost at all. New devices, search engines, cool apps, pricey programs, social networks, instant messengers, the list goes on. All are ways that journalists can quickly obtain information that they need to stay on top of their beats. But which apps or tools are must-haves? Which should you pay for? Must you be on every social network? Which ones matter the most?

This chapter focuses mainly on free or relatively cheap tools and plans that will help journalists find sources, spot trends and other story ideas, and verify the information they find online and via social media.

In their research article, "A Question of Power: The Changing Dynamics Between Journalists and Sources," Marcel Broersma, Bastiaan Den Herder,

 **Jax Sheriff's Office** ✓
@JSOPIO

 Follow ⌄

We are finding many people hiding in locked areas at The Landing. We ask you to stay calm, stay where you are hiding. SWAT is doing a methodical search inside The Landing. We will get to you. Please don't come running out. #TheLandingMassShooting

> **Jax Sheriff's Office** ✓ @JSOPIO
> Mass shooting at the Jacksonville Landing. Stay far away from the area. The area is not safe at this time. STAY AWAY #TheLandingMassShooting

11:55 AM - 26 Aug 2018

💬 106　　🔁 3.5K　　♡ 3.8K　　✉

Figure 8.3 Screenshot of 11:55 a.m. tweet from Jacksonville Sheriff's Office. Twitter.

Jax Sheriff's Office ✓
@JSOPIO

Follow ⌄

IMPORTANT If you are hiding in The Landing. Call 911 so we can get to you. #TheLandingMassShooting

> **Jax Sheriff's Office** ✓ @JSOPIO
> Mass shooting at the Jacksonville Landing. Stay far away from the area. The area is not safe at this time. STAY AWAY #TheLandingMassShooting

11:57 AM - 26 Aug 2018

💬 119　　🔁 5.4K　　♡ 5.2K　　✉

Figure 8.4 Screenshot of 11:57 a.m. tweet urging public to call 911 so they can get them. Twitter.

and Birte Schohaus write "news is born in a display of courtship between journalists and sources. The former has to seduce the latter to contribute to news stories, to give them information and to provide interesting and attractive quotes, preferably on the record."[1]

Sources, the authors add, are "indispensable to confirm and validate information that underlies news stories, even when shorter routine stories based on information subsidies are circulated without being thoroughly checked or checked at all."[2]

Politicians, company executives, public relations specialists, and others who desire positive news coverage are often seeking to be interviewed by journalists. In the past, they have sent **press releases** or called news organizations directly to alert them of possible stories. Nowadays, many more companies, **public relations (PR)** professionals, celebrities, and politicians are bypassing the news media and disseminating their messages straight to the public via the web and social media.

Perhaps that is why social media has become a critical element in a journalist's effort to stay on top of the news. It's fairly easy to find out what politicians, celebrities, and other people seeking news coverage are doing, and that's because nearly every major social network allows almost anyone to follow, friend, or connect with people at the highest levels of government, celebrities, athletes, and others around the world.

By following some or all of these newsmakers, journalists will learn rather quickly if they have tweeted or posted something that might be newsworthy.

For example, when President Trump tweeted at 5:03 a.m. on July 31, 2018 that he didn't think "3-D plastic guns made much sense," *USA Today* was among the many news outlets to report that his tweet came less than 24 hours before that technology was to become widely available.[3]

When the Instagram community erupted in criticism in July 2018 about reality TV star Kim Kardashian straightening her daughter's hair, the story

Donald J. Trump ✅
@realDonaldTrump

(Follow)   ⌄

I am looking into 3-D Plastic Guns being sold to the public. Already spoke to NRA, doesn't seem to make much sense!

5:03 AM - 31 Jul 2018

💬 20K   🔁 10K   ♡ 51K   ✉

Figure 8.5 Screenshot of tweet from President Trump on 3-D plastic guns. Twitter.

Figure 8.6 Screenshot of Kim Kardashian and her daughter with straight hair on Instagram. Instagram.

became top news for *People*, *Vogue*, *Cosmopolitan*, *Insider*, and many other lifestyle magazines.

Thus, it is clear that social media is a dominant factor in not only how the audience receives news and information, but how journalists decide which stories to pursue for their readers, viewers, and listeners – once again confirming how the traditional roles of gatekeepers and agenda-setters have evolved due to advances in technology and social media.

"So far, our research shows that journalists still use the mainstream social media channels like Facebook and Twitter to research and source their stories," Christopher Van Mossevelde wrote in his March 12, 2018 blog post on how journalists use social media.[4]

One easy way to know what newsmakers are saying on their websites, public newsletters, blogs, podcasts, and social media networks is to conduct regular searches of their names and other keywords associated to them. You can do this on Google and other search engines, and, in many cases, you can set up alerts that come directly to your laptop or phone.

Another way to know what public figures are saying is to find their public profiles on social media and follow them. Twitter is a good place to follow people because most accounts are public, she explains in her online Coursera class. It becomes a bit trickier on LinkedIn, where people are

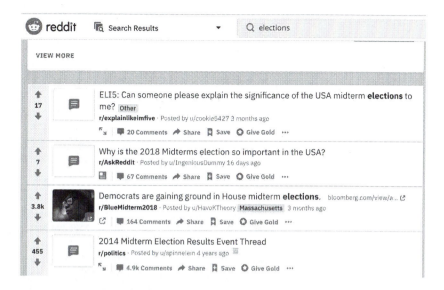

Figure 8.7 Screenshot of search for election stories on Reddit. Reddit.

advised to connect with those you know or Facebook, where people usually only connect with friends and family.

In cases where it may be awkward to connect with or "friend" celebrities and other people important to your beat, you can look for business or public accounts set up by celebrities and others – because these accounts will allow you to receive public posts or updates from them.

Another way to monitor the news is with Reddit.

Reddit

Reddit, one of the top visited websites in the United States, allows its registered members to submit content, which is then voted up or down by other members. The site name is a play on the words "I read it." As of spring 2018, Reddit had about 330 million monthly active users, according to the Digital Trends website.[5]

On a daily basis, Reddit sees 2.8 million comments and 58 million up or down votes. Young adults are the most active on the platform, with 79 percent of users falling in the 18 to 34 age group.

Stacey Leasca, a freelance journalist and former social media editor for the *Los Angeles Times*, told MediaShift in 2014 that she tracked trending news through search engines such as *Google* and Yahoo, but her favorite tool was Reddit, describing it as the "voice of the audience."[6]

Just before the *Breaking Bad* TV series ended in 2013, *The Wall Street Journal* social media team created a Google form and asked people via Twitter how they thought the "show should and would end. Hundreds of responses later, the team compiled the best ones in an article and had an illustrator bring a few answers to life."[7]

In a survey of nearly 100 students in Broadcast and Electronic Communication Arts (BECA) at San Francisco State University, a large number mentioned that Reddit is an invaluable source of news and information.

"I learned about the Florida shooting on Reddit, a forum-ish site that I use daily for my news, questions I have, or just to kill time," one student wrote in his essay. "I didn't check television news as I don't watch television, but most of the online news I did check from Reddit were redirect links to Fox News, CNN, and other small independent online news companies."

What makes Reddit a go-to place for so many young people?

In one word: interactivity. On Reddit, the audience is as important as the people who produce the stories themselves.

And this, some observers note, is one element sorely missing in traditional news outlets. Though most print and broadcast media outlets have added their stories to their websites, many have failed to engage their audience in any meaningful way, says Alice Hendricks and Misty McLaughlin.

"Instead of starting with channels, mediums, and devices, **Digital First** is a methodology—a new way of thinking and working," Hendricks and McLaughlin wrote in their 2016 article on the need to rethink what digital first means. "Digital First acknowledges that the digital landscape, and your audiences' expectations, will always be changing."[8] With so many platforms and sites to choose from, how do you stay on track of every post, tweet or conversation?

There are hundreds of strategies and cool tools and apps that you can use to find story ideas, gather information for your stories, and even diversify the viewpoints in your stories. The question is how much do you want to spend? Some programs can cost hundreds or even thousands of dollars each year. Luckily, there are some tools that cost next to nothing or are free.

Social Media Management Tools and Apps

TweetDeck, Buffer, and Hootsuite are among many social media management apps that can help journalists stay on top of the news.

TweetDeck, which was acquired by Twitter in 2011, is a free app that allows you to manage multiple Twitter accounts through a dashboard. You can arrange the columns by topics, people, hashtags, and so on – and you can also create columns for your notifications and direct messages.[9]

Hootsuite

Hootsuite is another social media management app. Its free version allows you to manage up to three social media accounts from one dashboard. For a cost, you can manage even more accounts, collaborate with teams, and get access to social analytics.[10]

Buffer

Buffer's free version lets you to schedule a certain number of posts for up to three social media accounts. For a cost, you can manage even more accounts and schedule even more posts at one time.[11]

In addition to social media management apps, you can set up news alerts that go to your laptop and/or phone.

Google Alerts

Google Alerts will alert you whenever **Google** finds your keywords on web pages, news articles, blogs, and so on. To set up an alert, you simply go to http://www.google.com/alerts/ and fill out the form, choosing keywords for your search and how often you want to be notified.

Apple News is a mobile app that curates news based on your interests. You can customize the settings to receive alerts.

While all of these tools will help journalists stay on top of so much information, it's important to remember the latest tools and apps come and go. The key thing is to figure out your own system of staying on top of the news.

The New York Times breaking news reporter Jonah Bromwich admits that he and other journalists at his news organization rely on a pricey program called Dataminr, which is used by more than 400 newsrooms to scour various social media platforms for relevant breaking news and then alerts its users via TweetDeck, Slack, email, mobile, and more.[12]

"Basically what it does is provide us with a continuously updating feed of tweets that have breaking news in them," Bromwich said in his April 11, 2018 column:

> For example, we could become aware of a story that we want to monitor (and possibly cover) when a tweet from a local Houston reporter says something like, "Gunshots fired in Harris County Institute of the Forensic Sciences." And then seconds later, another one from a different account says, "Whoa im in Houston and I think i just heard fireworks or maybe gunfire???[13]

As of fall 2018, Dataminr, which describes itself as a "real-time information discovery company," was only available as a paid product for companies, which is one great reason to work at *The New York Times* or other companies big enough to pay for the service.

Journalism Crowdsourcing

While using apps and tools that can help you stay on top of the news, these apps don't necessarily help you find people you need for every story. For example, if you're writing a story about families coming to the U.S. to escape violence in their home countries, they may not currently be in your networks. So, how do you find them?

One technique to find the people who are not in your network or who may not even have a social media account is to engage in **journalism crowdsourcing**.

The Tow Center for Digital Journalism defines journalism crowdsourcing as the "act of specifically inviting a group of people to participate in a reporting task—such as newsgathering, data collection, or analysis – through a targeted, open call for input; personal experiences; documents; or other contributions."[14]

The ability to crowdsource through Twitter and other social networks has helped journalists reach people who have no interest in talking to the news media, but are interested in sharing their stories with their friends, families, or connections. These folks could include victims of a natural disaster or crime, and people accused of wrongdoing, who rarely have an interest in talking to the media. Journalists know reaching these people and having them explain what happened is critical to great storytelling. This is where social media, websites, and blogs become indispensable.

And it's relatively easy to do, according to the Tow Center for Digital Journalism, which adds that crowdsourcing for journalists usually takes two forms:

- "An unstructured call-out, which is an open invitation to vote, email, call, or otherwise contact a journalist with information."
- "A structured call-out, which engages in targeted outreach to ask people to respond to a specific request. Responses can enter a newsroom via multiple channels, including email, SMS, a website, or Google form. Often, they are captured in a searchable database."[15]

The *Tow Center for Digital Journalism* has outlined six different calls to action when crowdsourcing.

We acknowledge that crowdsourcing efforts don't fit neatly into discrete classification, but for the prupose of this report, we've organized our typologies into six different calls to action:

- Voting—prioritizing which stories reporters should tackle.
- Witnessing—sharing what you saw during a news event.
- Sharing personal experiences—telling what you know about your life experience.
- Tapping specialized expertise—contributing data or unique knowledge.
- Completing a task—volunteering time or skills to help create a news story.
- Engaging audiences—joining in call-outs that can range from informative to playful.[16]

"In short, it has done just what the pundits predicted a decade ago: helped turn journalism into more of a conversation, rather than a one-way megaphone," the project leaders wrote in their Tow Center for Digital Journalism report on crowdsourcing. "Crowdsourcing also deserves credit for shaping journalism into more of an iterative process: as data or stories come in from contributors, reporters see new possibilities for their journalism—and news organizations see opportunities to incrementally publish those contributions in ways that tease out more."[17]

Social Media Groups

Another way to stay informed is by joining groups on Reddit, Facebook, LinkedIn, and so on. For example, if you're looking for a medical doctor who can talk about a resurgence in whooping cough, you may find your next best source in a group on one of these platforms.

Figure 8.8 Screenshot of About page on Facebook's Journalism page. Facebook.

There are also groups that allow journalists to exchange ideas and support one another.

Conducting Interviews via Social Media

Ideally, you will want to talk to your sources in person or by phone. But there are times when you'll need to reach people quickly and social media can be a good choice for that.

"Tweetiquette" for Interviews

In 2011, *Adweek* came up with a great list on how to conduct interviews on Twitter[18] – and some of the magazine's tips have stood the test of time, as you'll see here:

- Explain what you're looking for, and be honest if you're seeking other sources.
- Make it easy for people contact or connect with you.
- Explain why you've chosen them and tell them a little about your story or stories.

Because Facebook allows users to send messages to just about anyone, the best tip for journalists is to follow the "Tweetiquette" rules when sending a message for an interview request to potential sources on Facebook. It may be more difficult to conduct interviews on LinkedIn, where you can't even send a message to someone unless you're connected with them – or you pay for a premium account on LinkedIn.

Importance of Verification

Given the rise of fake news, it has become critical for journalists to proceed cautiously when gathering information or finding sources via social media and other online methods.

"Despite all of the benefits of social media, there are also some reasons to be cautious about it," according to Earth Journalism Network. "It can be difficult, for instance, to verify whether information on social networks is true, and whether people are who they say they are. Additionally, social media greatly increases the speed at which information is transmitted, at times at the cost of the accuracy of the information."[19]

Earth Journalism Network adds that information published online or via social media does not mean that its author intended journalists to read and report it.

In *The Elements of Journalism*, Bill Kovach and Tom Rosenstiel wrote that journalism's "essence is a discipline of verification."[20]

Bruce Koon, former news director at KQED Radio in San Francisco, says the only way to verify information is by talking to sources directly.

"Young people don't know how to pick up the phone," Koon said. "Social media can help you get the pulse. But if there is confusion going on, get on the phone."[21]

Tory Starr, social media director for WGBH-TV in Boston, said in her blog post on Medium, that journalists should verify all information found on social media.

"After about 90 seconds scrolling Twitter, seeing reports of shooters in the New York, New York Casino, explosives on the Strip, and multiple gunmen on the loose, I was confused and terrified," Starr said, recalling the first few minutes of a mass shooting in Las Vegas, where she and her husband were staying. "The social verification techniques that I've taught newsrooms and journalists back at the public media station in Boston weren't possible for me to do in seconds, much less from my phone with a rapidly dwindling battery. . . . The single source I would use that night was my sister, texting from her home in Seattle."[22]

1   Verify the authenticity of the account by cross-checking information.
2   Conduct a search on the person's name and/or business.
3   Check out the followers, friends, and connections.
4   Contact people via the platform they seem to favor.
5   When looking at a website, always go to the About page to find out correct spelling of names.
6   Screengrab important images and information.

How to Combat Misinformation

If you are trying to correct or respond to misinformation, Harvard University Professor Judith Donath, offers these tips:

- State the truth rather than repeat the falsehood.
- Use visuals to attract attention to your falsehood-fighting social media posts.
- Fight memes with memes: Create your own shareable fact-based memes, to counteract the false ones found on social media.
- Should you call a lie a lie? Have a conversation in your newsroom and be consistent.
- When responding to those who spread misinformation on social media, attack the misinformation, not the people.
- Focus on a positive message if you can find one, and recognize that people's emotions play a part in what they believe (or don't believe).[23]

"For journalism students today, it's really important to just be cautious and wary of everything we see online," says Alex Janin of NowThis. "The old journalism adage still applies, right? If your mother says she loves you, check it out."[24]

Recently, Janin said she saw a story circulating with tens of thousands of retweets that Meek Mill, a rapper, was getting out of prison. "I had friends tweeting about it and everybody was celebrating. And then, shortly after, there's an article saying, no, this is completely made up. And so I circulated that."[25]

The Verification Process

The five steps to follow to verify images, video, and text from the web or social medi are:

1   Look for the original source of an image or video. Often times, images are shared by numerous individuals with no credit to the actual photographer or videographer.

2   Once the originator of a video or image is located, check to see if the original has been altered from what you're seeing online or any of the social networks. If you discover that a photo or video has been altered in a tweet, blog post, or other social post, what should you do?

3   Text in status updates, tweets, or blog posts should also be checked out. Often, you can simply copy and paste text into a search engine to discover if it's been used elsewhere or written by someone else.

4   Look for the original source of an image or video. Also check to see whether text in a blog post is original, and whether anything has been plagiarized or fabricated.

In her June 2016 Medium blog post, Julie Comnes offers the following tips for journalists to follow when seeking to verify social media content:

• Check out a potential source before contact him or her. "Make sure that their online identity checks out. Avoid as your source someone whose account was made just days before you found their account, or someone whose Twitter timeline is otherwise sparse or incongruent."

• Choose your quotes wisely. "If you were writing a source about a nearby fire, you wouldn't just include quotes from anyone on the scene who is willing to talk to you about the fire. You'd look for someone with a good story, someone who's rational and mentally stable, someone who is at least relatively articulate and who can say something of value."

• If it seems too good to be true, it probably is. "Think through whether or not what the account is posting is a normal thing for that kind of person to post."[26]

At the summer 2018 Association of Alternative Newsmedia (AAN) conference in San Diego, Aaron Sharockman, executive director of PolitiFact, the largest fact-checking organization in the United States, said journalists must be willing to "fact check everyone."

"No one," said Sharockman, who has been with PolitiFact since 2010, should be "off limits." He added: "I remember when I was in college, the professor would say you had to have three sources," Sharockman said. "To build competence in your reporting, you have to do a lot of interviews. One of our reporters talked to 12 experts for a story."[27]

He also said to be sure to explain to your audience why you are checking someone else's facts or trying to debunk them. Most important, he added, "words matter."

While the process of checking things out can seem time-consuming and may even prevent you from being first, there are some tools that can make verification much easier, Janin says.

"There are countless verification tools that exist on the internet that are free," Janin says. "There are reverse image search tools, called *Tin-Eye, Verify, FotoForensics*. There are video verification tools, like *YouTube Date viewer*, which help young journalists, and even your average citizen, if you want to figure out whether an image that you're looking at is either falsified or this isn't the first time it's been circulated."

Janin adds: "And a really easy way, if you're not trying to use a bunch of tools to help verify something, is to just look at a time stamp. Look at location stamps. Look at the person whose tweeting or spreading this information, look at their profile. How long have they been using this platform? If they're new, or this is their first or second tweet, you're probably looking at something that's either fake or is a bot, or something like that." [28]

You can make the important process of verification even easier by establishing a process that you follow each time. Such a process is outlined in *Verification Handbook*,[29] written by journalists from BBC, ABC, and other media outlets. Journalists Craig Silverman and Rina Tsubaki offer a simple methodology to follow when verifying information online and social media, which include putting a plan in place for verification before disasters and breaking news occur and never parroting or trusting "sources whether they are witnesses, victims or authorities."

The Verification Handbook also lists steps to follow when verifying user-generated content (UGC), used to describe "any form of content such as video, blogs, discussion form posts, digital images, audio files, and other forms of media that was created by consumers or end-users of an online system or service and is publicly available to others [sic] consumers and end-users."[30] Among those tips? "Start from the assumption that the content is 'inaccurate or been scraped, sliced, diced, duplicated and/ or reposted with different context,'" the authors write, adding that it's important to obtain "permission from the author/originator to use the content (photos, videos, audio)."[31]

Conclusion

The power of social media allows journalists to go beyond their comfort zones and explore the world around them. By following a diverse group of people, a journalist can stay in the know and connect with community. And that's important when journalists seek to fulfill the No. 1 mission under the SPJ Code of Ethics, which is to seek truth and report it (see Chapter 4).

Discussion Questions

1   What tactics can you use to verify information online and via social media?
2   How do you find sources using social media?
3   Search for Alex Janin on Google. What comes up first? Check out her website. Do you think it does a good job showcasing her brand? Why or why not?

Notes

1 Marcel Broersma, Bastiaan Den Herder, and Birte Schohaus, "A Question of Power: The Changing Dynamics between Journalists and Sources," *Journalism Practice* Vol.7, Issue 4, August 1, 2013, pp. 388–395.
2 Ibid.
3 Deirdre Shesgreen and Josh Hafner, "Trump tweets skepticism about 3D-printable guns. But his administration cleared the way for them," *USA Today*, July 31, 2018, https://www.usatoday.com/story/tech/nation-now/2018/07/23/3-d-printing-guns-downloadable-gun-legal-august-1/820032002/, accessed July 31, 2018.
4 Christopher Van Mossevelde, "How Journalists Use Social Media to Source Stories and Disseminate News," Mynewsdesk, Learn, March 12, 2018 https://learn.mynewsdesk.com/en/how-journalists-use-social-media/, accessed July 30, 2018.
5 Hillary Grigonis, "Reddit Scatters In-Feed Sponsored Posts Inside its Mobile Apps," Digital Trends, March 15, 2018, https://www.digitaltrends.com/social-media/reddit-ads-promoted-posts/, accessed July 31, 2018.
6 Melanie Stone, "Social Media Editors in the Newsroom: what the Job is really like," MediaShift, March 17, 2014, http://mediashift.org/2014/03/social-media-editors-in-the-newsroom-what-the-job-is-really-like/, accessed July 30, 2018.
7 Ibid.
8 Alice Hendricks and Misty McLaughlin, "Becoming a Digital-First Organization," May 19, 2016, Non-profit Technology Conference. https://www.nten.org/article/becoming-digital-first-organization/, accessed on February 20, 2018.
9 Elise Moreau, "What is TweetDeck and is it Only for Twitter?" Lifewire, April 30, 2018, https://www.lifewire.com/is-tweetdeck-only-for-twitter-3486080, accessed July 28, 2018.
10 Elise Moreau, "What is Hootsuite and Is It Free?" Lifewire, July 5, 2018, https://www.lifewire.com/what-is-hootsuite-3486042, accessed July 28, 2018.

11 Elise Moreau, "Why You Should Use the Buffer App to Schedule Your Social Media Posts," Lifewire, April 3, 2018, https://www.lifewire.com/buffer-social-media-scheduling-3486540, accessed July 28, 2018.

12 Dataminr, https://www.dataminr.com/news.

13 Jonah Engel Bromwich, "How to Stay on Top of Breaking News," *The New York Times*, April 11, 2017, https://www.nytimes.com/2018/04/11/technology/personaltech/how-to-stay-on-top-of-breaking-news.html, accessed July 28, 2018.

14 Mimi Onuoha, Jeanne Pinder, and Jan Schaffer, "Guide to Crowdsourcing," Tow Center for Digital Journalism, November 20, 2015, https://towcenter.org/research/guide-to-crowdsourcing/, accessed August 1, 2018.

15 Ibid.

16 Ibid.

17 Ibid.

18 Meranda Adams, "How, When to Request Interviews on Twitter," *Adweek*, August 16, 2011, https://www.adweek.com/digital/how-when-to-request-interviews-on-twitter/, accessed July 30, 2018.

19 Earth Journalism Network, "Using Social Media," June 9, 2016, https://earthjournalism.net/resources/using-social-media, accessed July 31, 2018.

20 Bill Kovach and Tom Rosenstiel, *The Elements of Journalism*, London, Penguin, 2001.

21 Author's interview with Koon, spring 2018.

22 Tory Starr, "This social media journalist turned away from social during the Las Vegas shooting," Medium, October 4, 2017, https://medium.com/@torystarr3/this-social-media-journalist-turned-away-from-social-during-the-las-vegas-shooting-facbc397d3e3.

23 Jane Elizabeth, American Press Institute, https://www.americanpressinstitute.org/publications/reports/strategy-studies/reinventing-social-team/.

24 Author's interview with Alex Janin, spring 2018.

25 Ibid.

26 Julie Comnes, "Four Tips for Using Social Media Sources Wisely, June 12, 2016, https://medium.com/social-media-for-journalists/four-tips-for-using-social-media-sources-wisely-64ada844e6c6, accessed March 26, 2019.

27 During a panel discussion at the AAN conference in 2018.

28 Author's interview with Alex Janin, spring 2018.

29 Craig Silverman (Ed.), *The Verification Handbook*, London, European Journalism Centre (EJC), 2014.

30 Jonathan D. James, "The Internet and the Google age, https://files.eric.ed.gov/fulltext/ED576697.pdf, accessed March 26, 2019.

31 Chapter 9 of the *Verification Handbook*, http://verificationhandbook.com/book/chapter9.php, accessed March 26, 2019.

~st Practices for Curating and Creating Content for and With Digital and Social Media

Figure 9.1 Illustration of content creation. Getty Images.

Content Curation

Social media has changed every aspect of journalism, from finding sources to the dissemination of news. When people share news and information via blog posts and social media networks, they are often curating content. **Content curation** is defined as the act of "discovering, gathering, and presenting digital content that surrounds specific subject matter."[1]

Curation can take the form of "links posted on blogs, social media feeds, or an online news mashup like the ECDaily (The EContent Daily)," wrote

Eileen Mullan in her 2011 article defining content creation in. "There are no limits when it comes to the types of content either. Videos, articles, pictures, songs, or any piece of online digital content that can be shared can be curated."[2]

Content curation has been used for years by marketers, companies, bloggers and others interested in driving **Search Engine Optimization** (SEO). That's because Google and other search engines have rewarded sites that link to multiple pieces on the same subject.

Content curation has other SEO and brand-building benefits,[3] including the ability be seen as a thought leader or expert in your field, according to the content marketing team at Brafton.

Curating content on social media, however, can be time-consuming, especially if done well. That's why a lot of companies, including some news entities and individual journalists and bloggers, use content curation tools. Tools, of course, are constantly changing, but a couple of good ones for the moment include Curata, a content curation system that start at nearly $500 a month, and Pocket, which allows people to save shareable content and share them whenever they want.

Entertainment blogger Perez Hilton, for example, offers his own take on the images and video he collects from other magazines, the web and social media. Hilton, who started his own blog in 2004 with very little money, reportedly now has a net worth of $30 million.[4]

An example follows of how Hilton finds and curates content from social media or other websites to use on his hugely successful site, which reportedly makes most of its money through sponsorships.[5]

Content Creation

Content creation differs from content curation because it means you are creating original content for various platforms. While this could be quite time-consuming for others, journalists trained in this craft can be masters at content creation, which refers to the act of creating and promoting your own content.[6]

The difference today is that journalists must create content in a variety of ways, everything from the 6 o'clock news to the front page, the home page, the newsroom blog, to podcasts, social media accounts, newsletters, and much more.

These days, journalists are expected to do it all. While they can certainly produce quality content, many have not quite figured out how to optimize their content to attract and engage their target audience, without posting something funny or outrageous.

So, how should journalists create content for social and digital media? Remember the basic SPJ ethical principles: seek truth, minimize harm, act independently, and be transparent. In other words, be authentic, kind to others, avoid gifts, and communicate with your audience.

The good news is this: the demand for real-time news has never been greater. Indeed, a journalist that happens to be at a scene of a crime or other

ZHILTON PEREZTV GALLERI

Home › Galleries › Kylie Jenner's Top Beauty Secrets

Baking To Shape

Kylie can't do her makeup without baking her face, especially along her jaw line AFTER contouring with bronzer to keep things looking defined and bright.

[Image via Kylie Jenner/Instagram.]

Figure 9.2 Screenshot of Perez Hilton's post curating content about Kylie from her Instagram account. Website.

breaking news story is pretty much expected to start reporting the news via social media. A good example of this is when a lone gunman opened fire in the *Capital Gazette* newsroom in Annapolis, Maryland, killing five employees, some of whom were news reporters. Though the situation was chaotic and frightening for the people at the scene, journalist Phil Davis immediately tweeted the situation out to the public.

The ability to report news and engage with the audience via social media is another reason why newsrooms are hopeful about the future. For example, revenue from the digital-only subscriptions to *The New York Times*,

Phil Davis
@PhilDavis_CG

There is nothing more terrifying than hearing
multiple people get shot while you're under
your desk and then hear the gunman reload

12:46 PM - 28 Jun 2018 from Maryland, USA

◯ 2.2K   ⟲ 24K   ♡ 54K   ✉

Figure 9.3 Screenshot of tweets from Phil Davis during the *Capital Gazette*
shooting in June 2018. Twitter.

known as "The Gray Lady," has skyrocketed, buoyed by the perception of
unbiased reporting during the 2016 presidential election and groundbreaking reporting of the Harvey Weinstein sexual harassment story.[7] In 2017,
The Wall Street Journal added 300,000 digital subscriptions.[8]

Trust is also up at some major news publications, according to a 2017
University of Missouri survey of 8,728 people.[9] The survey found that the
most-trusted was *The Economist* and Occupy Democrats were the least trusted.

The survey also confirmed that there is a connection between a person's
race, age, and political leanings and trust in particular people or news outlets.

"We found, for example, that users who mentioned Rachel Maddow
as trusted were more liberal than average, while users who trust Rush
Limbaugh were more conservative than average," Joy Mayer said about
the report. "Liberals most often cited *The New York Times*, NPR and *The
Washington Post* as trusted, while the brand most listed by conservatives was
Fox News."[10]

The survey also found that more than two-thirds of respondents said they
provided financial support to at least one news organization.[11]

While it is heartening to hear that people trust and pay for traditional
news stories, it's important to understand that the first place many people,
especially young people, turn to for news is NOT the local news station
or cable news. A student in my Broadcast and Electronic Communication
Arts (BECA) 460 class, a class of nearly 100 students in spring 2018, said
she heard about the shooting at Stoneman Douglas High in Florida from a
friend and then scrolled down her Facebook newsfeed to learn more.

Another student said that he learned about the Florida shooting "through
my group chat." The same student added: "I think Twitter probably did
the best job as far as breaking news, and I think the follow up coverage
was mostly fine except for the stuff that started to attempt to determine the
shooter's political motives."

So, how can journalists create content that is seen by their target audience? The first step is to understand how the audience engages with media.

Under the Uses and Gratification Theory (introduced in Chapter 1), the audience "has power over their media consumption and assumes an active role in interpreting and integrating media into their own lives."[12]

Uses and Gratification Theory researchers have grouped the audience's goals for media into five uses:

1   To be informed or educated.
2   To identify with characters of the situation in the media environment.
3   To be entertained.
4   To enhance social interaction.
5   To escape from the stresses of daily life.

1)   Audience need: To be informed and educated

For the news media, journalists have the opportunity to meet at least one of the audience's needs, which is to educate and inform the public. While newsrooms may not be the first to inform the public about a shooting on a street corner or an earthquake in Indonesia, they are usually the ones to provide accurate information about natural disasters, political races, and more. Thus, the news media can be seen as doing a good job of fulfilling the audience's need to be informed and educated.

2)   Audience need: To identify with characters of the situation in the media environment

Journalists learned long ago that if you want someone to care about a threatened increase in taxes, it was best to feature a person who would be affected, and show how it would affect them in the lead. This is known as an **anecdotal lead**, which essentially means the person or issue described in the lead or top of the story exemplifies a problem that affects a lot more people. This type of lead and story allows the audience to connect with the story because many can relate to or identify with the person in the story, thus fulfilling the second need of the audience under the Uses and Gratification Theory.

3)   Audience need: To be entertained

While not every news story will entertain the audience, many will. Stories about sports, Hollywood, recreation, music, and so on can not only inform the audience, but also entertain those who have not had a chance to check out a concert, for example. And depending on how you write the story, some pieces (such as humor columns) can be much more entertaining than others.

4)   **Audience need: To enhance social interaction**

In the old days, newsrooms didn't worry too much about social interaction because they were often the gatekeepers of news. The audience waited until a certain hour for their paper or news show, and then were told what the news was. There was little opportunity for the public to offer feedback, other than the occasional letter to the editor. But as we learned earlier in this book, the world wide web and social media have changed all that. The audience not only wants to engage with information and news, they want to contribute, and many do as citizen journalists.

An increasing number of digital-first companies have figured out how to create some content that enhances social interaction, but, in general, most newsrooms and journalists have a much harder time creating content that encourages social interaction.

5)   **Audience need: To escape from the stresses of daily life**

In general, front-page or top-of-the-hour news tends to be serious, sobering, and sometimes gloomy. So, it's no surprise that newsrooms and journalists have a tough time creating content that allows the audience to escape from the stresses of daily life.

However, newsrooms have been masters at telling stories about fun vacation spots, new concerts, popular culture, entertainment, sports, and much more for a very long time. Think about the different sections of the paper: Sports, Entertainment, Lifestyle, Books, and so on. These lighter stories are indeed ways for people to have fun or relax.

The challenge nowadays is deciding how much "fluff" a traditional newsroom or journalist should post on social media. One way to do that is to use the 80–20 rule. For every four pieces of hard-hitting news stories, give your followers and connections two fun pieces.

Another way to do that is to create **verticals** that take a much lighter approach to news and information. A vertical is simply defined as a type of publication "whereby the content is primarily focused on one particular type of business or industry."[13] Buzzfeed does a great job of creating verticals that show off its humorous, quirky, and lighter sides. Yet Buzzfeed also has a strong news vertical with 250 reporters covering the world.

"We cover what you care about, break big stories that hold major institutions accountable for their actions, and expose injustices that change people's lives," editors wrote on the About Page for Buzzfeed News, which launched in 2012. "A BuzzFeed News story freed a man from prison. We have exposed the attempts to hide the death toll in Puerto Rico after Hurricane Maria, exploitative content on internet platforms, and the secrets of government officials from London to São Paulo."[14]

Newer news outlets such as Buzzfeed News aren't the only ones developing a vertical content strategy, which is defined as a holistic approach to

Figure 9.4 Screenshot of Buzzfeed News page, November 8, 2018. Buzzfeed.com.

content that takes "one part of that whole – a section, a specific topic, a content type – and delves into it across not only channels (websites, social media channels, print, events, etc.) but possibly a wider spectrum of audiences as well (particularly audiences within firewalls like internal sales or channel partners)."[15]

The New Yorker has launched web channels dedicated to science, technology, business, culture, humor, and more. "The digital push has resulted in major audience and ad revenue growth," publisher Lisa Hughes said in a 2013 *Adweek* article.[16]

The New York Times also has a number of verticals, focusing on streaming content, health, and wellness. Its cooking vertical has more than eight million visitors monthly.[17] "The biggest thing we learned from Cooking is that *The New York Times*' authority, and trust that people have in our brand, can be applied in meaningful ways," *New York Times Beta* vice president Ben French told Digiday.[18]

In 2017, NBC News created a vertical on the media, naming Claire Atkinson from *The New York Post* as the lead for "internal and external contributors to cover the media industry for all of NBC News and MSNBC's broadcast and digital platforms."[19]

In June 2018, Gannett, the publisher of *USA Today*, launched *USA & Main*, describing it as a service journalism hub for small-business owners and an "ad-supported part of *USA Today*'s Money vertical."[20]

"Any time we're experimenting with new verticals where we had pre-existing expertise, that cross-pollination effect, we're able to achieve critical mass," Michael Kuntz, president of ad sales and partnerships for the *USA Today* Network, told Digiday. "We believe we can very quickly scale."[21]

Another important thing to consider when posting to social media is the **customer journey**.

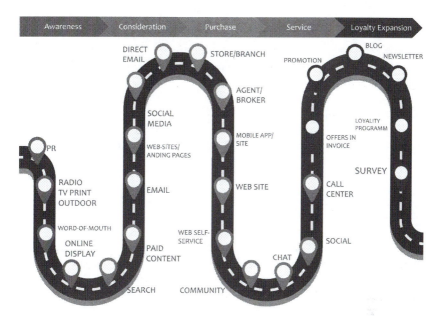

Figure 9.5 Customer journey map. https://www.istockphoto.com/vector/customer-journey-map-gm822887058-133225145

The customer journey is defined as the "complete sum of experiences that customers go through when interacting with your company and brand."[22]

As you can see from the customer journey map, social media can help with the awareness of a product or service, and once again when a potential customer is checking out the company or person's brand or reputations and at the end, when the customer who has bought the product or service wants to offer reviews to others.

For journalists, understanding the customer journey means that it's important to showcase your work on social media to raise awareness about your work. It is also important that others are talking about your work and sharing their praise with others so that people thinking about tuning into the show or paying for a subscription see a strong brand or reputation developed. At the end of the journey, newsrooms and journalists should attempt to turn their readers, viewers, and listeners into advocates, by offering them discounts, freebies, and, of course, quality product, so they can tell others to check you out as well.

"The underlying strategy is to meet customers and readers where they are in relationship to our brands and then have a 'conversation' that helps them choose how to engage next. Again, this is another basic principle," says Laura Inman, senior director of Audience Engagement at Cox Media Group newspapers.[23]

How to Increase Social Interaction

No matter how many verticals or types of content you have for your blog or news site, it's important to create online content that will grab the attention of your target audience. One way to do that is to generate buzz around your articles.

And you can do that through social interaction, meaning that your followers and connections share your content to an even larger audience.

Four Ways for News Companies to Increase Social Interaction

1) LiveChat

LiveChat is an offline customer service software developed by LiveChat Software.[24]

"Sending an email to customer support may still work for some people but many customers are in need of instant gratification," Kenny Tripura of Edkent Media said in a post for *Forbes* magazine. "Using live chat allows your company to connect to the customer on the spot as the visitor continues to browse your website."[25]

2) Content marketing

Content marketing is defined as a strategic marketing approach focused on "creating and distributing valuable, relevant, and consistent content to attract and retain a clearly defined audience — and, ultimately, to drive profitable customer action."[26] In other words, content marketing means writing helpful blogs and/or social media posts that educate your potential customer about your products or services – instead of trying to sell to them directly.

"The belief is that your audience over time will come to trust and rely on your guidance, recognize your company's unique value proposition, and ultimately reward you with business and loyalty," the Content Marketing Institute's Jodi Harris.[27]

3) Email marketing

Email marketing essentially means targeting consumers through email. "Although email has been around for a long time, email marketing is still a cost-effective way to promote your company – if you use the proper method," according to Tripura.[28]

4) Social media marketing (SMM)

Social media marketing is simply defined as the use of social media to market a company's products and services.[29]

"According to a Deloitte Consulting report, when social media is part of the buyer's journey, customers are 29 percent more likely to a purchase on the same day," Tripura writes. "The customer's spending levels also increase four times compared to those without a social component. It's the overall engagement levels that social media platforms provide that make them such powerful digital marketing tools."[30]

NOTE: Even though many of these tips apply to any business seeking to sell a product or service, they can work for newsrooms and journalists who seek to build new readers, viewers, and listeners – and eventually convert some of those loyal fans into subscribers and donors.

Fun Facts to Know About Content on Social Media

- Tweets with images get 18 percent more clicks, 89 percent more likes, and 150 percent more retweets.[31]
- Photos on Facebook receive 5 percent more likes than the average post and attract 104 percent more comments.[32]
- 81 percent of people only skim the content they read online.[33]
- An estimated 84 percent of communications will be visual by 2018.[34]
- An estimated 79 percent of internet traffic will be video content by 2018.[35]

The Importance of Headlines

Increasing social interaction is important for reaching your target audience, but nothing will grab them like a great headline. Think back to the old days before we were all on our phones and mobile devices. Between the 1890s and 1940s, newspaper boys were hired to yell, "Extra, Extra! Read all about it!"[36] The idea was to entice passers-by to stop and buy the newspaper.

Fast forward to the 21st century. While it remains important to grab someone's attention, there are very few newspapers being sold on the street corners of America. Indeed, as the Pew Research Center pointed out, an increasing number of people are scrolling pretty briskly through their newsfeeds to learn about what's happening around them.

So, how do you get them to stop scrolling? The Uses and Gratification Theory says one of the five needs of the audience is to be informed. So, you want to write a headline that informs, but more importantly, you want your audience to stay long enough on your headline that they will want to know more. As advertising legend David Ogilvy said: "On the average, five times as many people read the headline as read the body copy."[37]

Even if you manage to convince your audience to read the headline on your website, here's a sobering fact: 80 percent of your visitors will read your headline – but only 20 percent will go on to finish the article.[38]

That is why the headline you write for social and digital media is so important. The key, however, is that many of the rules you learned about writing headlines for a print publication won't work in this space.

Figure 9.6 Newspaper boy. https://www.istockphoto.com/vector/
paperboy-gm695313712-128647945. Credit: Hanna Ferentc.

While a straightforward headline such as "Dog saves boy" might be good
enough to entice the audience to care about your story, it most likely will not
convince the user to take your desired action, which is to click on the link
and go to the news site. Why not? You've given away the punchline. And
this means that users will most likely keep scrolling down their newsfeed.

So, how do you get them to open up the link?

Business coach Michael Masterson has developed four basic rules to writing attention-grabbing headlines,[39] which can be very helpful to even the
most serious journalist, especially anyone seeking to capture the attention of
users of digital and social media. And they are:

- Make the headline unique.
- Be ultra-specific.

- It should convey a sense of urgency.
- Your headline has to be useful.

To break that down even further, try to answer these questions when writing headlines for digital and social media:

1   Does your headline give everything away? If your headline tells everyone the ending, why would they need to read the whole story? Remember, you want to drive traffic back to your site!
2   What value or benefit does your story offer? In other words, what will your potential reader, listener, or viewer get by checking out your story? Let them know in the headline.
3   What are the specific takeaways from your story? In other words, give your audience numbers that are easy to understand. Avoid vague words. Studies show that headlines with numbers tend to generate 73 percent more social share and engagement.[40]
4   Does your story evoke strong emotions?

"We found that the most virally shared articles have headlines with an average EMV score of 30 on the dot," says web guru Neil Patel. "At this point, most people ask, "what's EMV and how do I calculate it? If you're wondering, EMV stands for emotional marketing value, and the score is calculated by inserting your headline into a series of algorithms that compare your headline with the highest emotion-triggering words in the English vocabulary."[41]

Coschedule also has a free tool that analyzes everything from the emotional value to the optimal length of your headline.

No matter what tool you use or don't use, the most important thing when creating headlines in digital and social media is to find a way to convince

Figure 9.7 Screenshot of Coschedule's free headline analyzer tool. https://coschedule.com/headline-analyzer. Credit: Larryrains.

someone to want to learn "all about it," as the news boys used to say in the old days. "Headlines are lifelines to our readers," writes Vicki Krueger in a June 2017 article for *Poynter*. "They grab attention, build trust and help time-pressed consumers focus on the stories they care most about."[42]

Activity: Choose the Best Headline

"Donald Trump correct that 1 in 4 working-age Americans not employed"
  or
  "Donald Trump correct that very few working-age Americans not employed"
  "In a Small Town, People, Mysterious Disappearance Turns Neighbor Against Neighbor"
  or
  "In a Town of 11 People, Mysterious Disappearance Turns Neighbor Against Neighbor"
  In pairs or groups, discuss which headlines are better and explain why.

Blogging

Blogging, which has been around since the 1990s, initially "involved a personal web log, in which a person would journal about their day. From 'web log' came the term 'blog'."[43]

And it remains popular to this day, with more than 409 million people reading blogs on a regular basis, largely because text remains a powerful way to drive traffic to your paid services or products.[44]

There are many benefits to blogging – one is the ability to improve SEO. "Every good content marketer knows that blogs should serve the audience first, and the machine second," according to the marketing team at Flockler. "Yet, the blog is still a great way to help your business rank well from an SEO standpoint. But, this isn't an excuse for stuffing keywords into every article, the content has to please the reader. When it does that, it will be successful on Google too."[45]

Blogging, when it first arrived, was not seen as direct competition, and many newsrooms steered clear of the personalization of news. However, the number of newsroom blogs that offer an edgier and much more personalized view of news continues to increase.

Newsrooms see blogging and vlogging as a way to compete in the digital space, and they also see it as a way to connect with a younger generation and offer a more casual take on the news through opinion and humor.

Figure 9.8 llustration by Ashley DeLeon. © The Balance, 2018.
https://www.thebalancesmb.com/blogging-what-is-it-1794405

The key for journalists when blogging is to remember that it's also part of your personal brand. And what you say in a blog, even one meant solely for friends and family, will help define how the public perceives you. If you choose to write about how much you love your Apple iPhone, it will be hard to convince the public that you will be fair in your review a new Samsung product. Remember what the SPJ Code of Ethics says: "Avoid conflicts of interest, real or perceived. Disclose unavoidable conflicts."[46]

Starting a blog has gotten easier and cheaper over the years. You can start a blog for free on a **content management system** (CMS) such as Blogger, but WordPress is considered the leading CMS platform, running on more than 15 million websites.[47] You can even posts blogs directly from social networks such as LinkedIn, Tumblr, and Medium.

The content you create for your blog can also be "broken down into bite-sized pieces to socialize on differing channels."[48]

The most important thing about blogging, however, is to be consistent.

Vlogging

Video blogging, or **vlogging**, is an increasingly popular way to produce news and offer perspectives on important issues for a digital audience, especially a younger audience much more attuned to visual storytelling. The Cisco Visual Networking Index predicts that by 2021, video traffic will make up 82 percent of all consumer internet traffic. That's up from 73 percent in 2016.[49]

The "vlog has become the richest source of information, knowledge, as well as internet entertainment," according to a 2018 article by *Digital Dimensions*. "If you want to understand the popularity of vlog, just Google it, and you will be amazed that many people prefer to source information through video content than any other thing else. This goes to prove the findings from various studies that more people prefer to sit down and watch videos than to read five hundred to six hundred words blog posts and so on."[50]

John Lynch of Business Insider Nordic said in his 2018 report that YouTube has become the "de facto launchpad for the next generation of celebrities" since 2005.[51]

"From comedians to gamers to vloggers of all kinds, YouTubers have generally built their followings outside of the control of media giants, even if they are now signing big deals with those companies," Lynch said in his article. "And there is power and independence in having that huge fan base."[52]

Podcasting

The number of Americans who listen to **podcasts** has nearly doubled from 12 percent of the U.S. population in 2013 to 24 percent in 2017. Merriam-Webster defines a podcast is a "program (as of music or talk) made available in digital format for automatic download over the Internet."

The biggest group of listeners of podcasts are millennials. In fact, of the 68 million listeners in 2017, 44 percent were between the ages of 18 and 34.[53]

Marketing expert Sidney Pierucci attributes the popularity of podcasting to an "unusual sense of intimacy, the ability to productively multitask while driving or working out and great stories–the power of narrative."[54]

Understanding the power of podcasts, a growing number of newsrooms now offer their own brand of podcasts. *The New York Times* has a successful podcast called "The Daily," and NPR has a slew of successful podcast that include: "This American Life," "Serial," and "Hidden Brain." [55]

How to Create a Podcast

There are numerous ways to learn how to create a podcast. You can go to a formal workshop, take classes, watch online tutorials, or learn from a friend. There are also various tools that can take the headache out of learning complicated programs for editing sound.

But the basics of a podcast are these:

1   Decide your topic and come up with a unique name (think about your personal brand).
2   Decide how often you want to air your podcast.

3   Choose your format and equipment.
4   Publish your podcast to iTunes and other places.

Conclusion

Journalists are among the best content creators in the world, but new apps and tools can make their jobs a lot easier. By learning how to create and curate meaningful and compelling content, an increasing number of newsrooms are finding ways to stand out and increase their digital subscriptions. The key, however, is to balance the public's desire to be entertained with their need to know important stories. And that is the balance that newsrooms and journalists will continue to confront as they seek to create and curate the right mix of information and news for the public.

Notes

1   Eileen Mullan, "What is Content Creation?" *EContent Magazine*, November 30, 2011, http://www.econtentmag.com/Articles/Resources/Defining-EContent/What-is-Content-Curation-79167.htm, accessed August 1, 2018.
2   Eileen Mullan, "What is Content Creation?" November 30, 2011, EContent, http://www.econtentmag.com/Articles/Resources/Defining-EContent/What-is-Content-Curation-79167.htm, accessed March 28, 2019.
3   Brafton, "Content creation in 2018: When, Why, and How," May 24, 2018, https://www.brafton.com/blog/distribution/content-curation-in-2018-when-why-how/, accessed July 31, 2018.
4   Celebrity Net Worth, https://www.celebritynetworth.com/richest-celebrities/perez-hilton-net-worth/.
5   Blogging.com, "How much do the top bloggers earn?" https://blogging.com/top-bloggers/.
6   Margot da Cunha, "The 7 best content curation tools in 2017," Wordstream, March 23, 2018, https://www.wordstream.com/blog/ws/2017/05/01/content-curation-tools, accessed August 1, 2018.
7   Laharee Chatterjee, "New York Times Beats as Digital Subscriptions Surge, Shares Rise," Reuters, February 8, 2018, https://www.reuters.com/article/us-new-york-times-results/new-york-times-beats-as-digital-subscriptions-surge-shares-rise-idUSKBN1FS249.
8   Todd Barish, "Why Subscription-based News is the Future," Odwyerpr.com, April 23, 2018, http://www.odwyerpr.com/story/public/10534/2018-04-23/why-subscription-based-news-is-future.html, accessed July 20, 2018.
9   Joy Mayer, "Who trusts – and pays for – the news? Here's what 8,728 people told us," Donald W. Reynolds Journalism Institute, July 27, 2017, https://www.rjionline.org/stories/who-trusts-and-pays-for-the-news-heres-what-8728-people-told-us?link=mktw, accessed July 20, 2018.
10 Ibid.
11 Ibid.
12 Hans-Juergen Strichow, *Our Ultimate Purpose in Life: The Grand Order of Design and the Human Condition*, Balboa Press, November 5, 2013, https://goo.gl/EgxqLx, accessed August 8, 2018.
13 Businessdictionary.com, http://www.businessdictionary.com/definition/vertical-publication.html

14 Buzzfeed News, https://www.buzzfeednews.com/article/buzzfeednews/about-buzzfeed-news

15 Lise Bissonnette Janody, "Global Content Insights, Horizontal and Vertical Content Strategy," Dot.connection, July 31, 2015, http://www.dot-connection.com/blog/horizontal-and-vertical-content-strategy, accessed August 8, 2018.

16 Emma Bazilian, "*New Yorker* to Launch New Online Verticals: Former Buzzfeed Editor to Oversee Tech Content," *Adweek*, January 31, 2013, https://www.adweek.com/digital/new-yorker-launch-new-online-verticals-146931/, accessed August 8, 2018.

17 Jordan Valinksy, "*The New York Times* is Launching a Television Website, Expanding Well," Digiday, March 10, 2016, https://digiday.com/media/new-york-times-launching-television-website-expanding-well/, accessed August 8, 2018.

18 Ibid.

19 Sara Guaglione, "NBC News Creates Dedicated Media Vertical," Mediapost, September 15, 2017, https://www.mediapost.com/publications/article/307408/nbc-news-creates-dedicated-media-vertical.html, accessed August 8, 2018.

20 Max Willens, "USA Today targets entrepreneurs with USA & Main," Digiday, July 31, 2018, https://digiday.com/media/usa-today-targets-entrepreneurs-usa-main/, accessed August 8, 2018.

21 Ibid.

22 Audra Sorman, "The best way to map the customer journey: take a walk in their shoes," Survey Monkey, https://www.surveymonkey.com/curiosity/map-customer-journey-keep-customers-happy/, accessed August 10, 2018.

23 Laura Inman, "Cox Media focuses lead-generation marketing efforts on customer journey," International News Media Association, August 22, 2017, https://www.inma.org/blogs/main/post.cfm/cox-media-focuses-lead-generation-marketing-efforts-on-customer-journey, accessed August 10, 2018.

24 LiveChat, https://www.livechatinc.com/why-livechat/

25 Kenny Tripura, "Four Ways to Increase Your Company's Interaction and Engagement Levels," *Forbes*, August 1, 2017, https://www.forbes.com/sites/forbesagencycouncil/2017/08/01/four-ways-to-increase-your-companys-interaction-and-engagement-levels/#16d135494a30, accessed August 9, 2018.

26 Content Marketing Institute, https://contentmarketinginstitute.com/what-is-content-marketing/

27 Jodi Harris, "Road Map to Success: Resources to Refresh Your Content Marketing Program," Content Marketing Institute, February 6, 2018, https://contentmarketinginstitute.com/2018/02/resources-content-marketing-success/, accessed August 9, 2018.

28 Kenny Tripura, "Four Ways to Increase Your Company's Interaction and Engagement Levels," *Forbes*, August 1, 2017, https://www.forbes.com/sites/forbesagencycouncil/2017/08/01/four-ways-to-increase-your-companys-interaction-and-engagement-levels/#16d135494a30, accessed March 27, 2019.

29 Investopedia, https://www.investopedia.com/terms/s/social-media-marketing-smm.asp

30 Ibid.

31 Shea Bennett, "Tweets with Images Get 18% More Clicks, 89% More Favorites and 150% More Retweets [STUDY], *Adweek*, https://www.adweek.com/digital/twitter-images-study/, accessed Nov. 8, 2018.

32 Rebecca Corliss, "Photos on Facebook Generate 53% More Likes Than the Average Post [NEW DATA]," https://blog.hubspot.com/blog/tabid/6307/bid/

33800/photos-on-facebook-generate-53-more-likes-than-the-average-post-new-data.aspx, accessed March 28, 2019.

33 Larry Kim, "16 Visual Content Marketing Statistics That Will Wake You Up," Medium, https://medium.com/marketing-and-entrepreneurship/16-visual-content-marketing-statistics-that-will-wake-you-up-59c4c0b80465, accessed Nov. 8, 2018.

34 Ibid.

35 Ibid.

36 TVTtropes.com, https://tvtropes.org/pmwiki/pmwiki.php/Main/ExtraExtra ReadAllAboutIt

37 Devedge, https://devedge-internet-marketing.com/2012/03/02/80-cents-of-dollar-spent-writing-headlines/

38 Neil Patel, "The step-by-step guide to writing headlines," https://neilpatel.com/blog/the-step-by-step-guide-to-writing-powerful-headlines/, accessed August 8, 2018.

39 Keyhole, https://keyhole.co/blog/the-guide-to-writing-marketing-headlines-with-examples-formulas/

40 Neil Patel, "The step-by-step guide to writing headlines," https://neilpatel.com/blog/the-step-by-step-guide-to-writing-powerful-headlines/, accessed August 8, 2018.

41 Neil Patel, "The step-by-step guide to writing headlines," https://neilpatel.com/blog/the-step-by-step-guide-to-writing-powerful-headlines/, accessed March 28, 2019.

42 Vicki Krueger, "9 tips for writing stronger headlines," *Poynter Institute,* June 6, 2017, https://www.poynter.org/news/9-tips-writing-stronger-headlines, accessed August 10, 2018.

43 Randy Duermyer, "What is blogging and why is it popular?" The Balance Small Business, July 31, 2018, https://www.thebalancesmb.com/blogging-what-is-it-1794405, accessed August 1, 2018.

44 Mary Nolan, "How to start a successful blog," The Balance Small Business, April 2, 2018, https://www.thebalancesmb.com/starting-successful-blog-2531526, accessed August 3, 2018.

45 Flocklr, "8 reasons why you still need a blog," https://flockler.com/blog/8-rea sons-why-you-still-need-to-blog, accessed March 28, 2019.

46 SPJ Code of Ethics, https://www.spj.org/ethicscode.asp.

47 Leslie Truex, "10 steps to setting up a wordpress self-hosted website", July 31, 2018, The Balance Small Business, https://www.thebalancesmb.com/steps-to-build-wordpress-website-4134417, accessed August 4, 2018.

48 Flocklr, "8 reasons why you still need a blog," https://flockler.com/blog/8-rea sons-why-you-still-need-to-blog.

49 Cisco Visual Networking Index: Forecast and Methodology, 2016–2021, https://www.cisco.com/c/en/us/solutions/collateral/service-provider/visual-networking-index-vni/complete-white-paper-c11-481360.html, accessed August 4, 2018.

50 Digital Dimensions, "Why you should start a Vlog in 2018," January 14, 2018, https://digitaldimensions4u.com/why-you-should-start-a-vlog-in-2018/, accessed March 28, 2019.

51 John Lynch, "These are the 19 most popular YouTube stars in the world — and some are making millions," Business Insider Nordic, February 2, 2018, https://

nordic.businessinsider.com/most-popular-youtubers-with-most-subscribers-2018-2?r=US&IR=T, accessed August 4, 2018.

52 Ibid.

53 Rose Leadem, "The Growth of Podcast and Why it Matters," *Entrepreneur*, December 23, 2017, https://www.entrepreneur.com/article/306174, accessed August 6, 2018.

54 Sidney Pierucci, "The rise of podcast and why 'YOU' should start one," March 8, 2018, https://medium.com/swlh/the-rise-of-podcast-and-why-you-should-start-one-48e10a17b79e, accessed August 4, 2018.

55 Top Podcast, http://toppodcast.com/

10 Promoting Your Content

Journalists seeking to uncover corruption at the highest levels of government or right the wrongs in society are quite courageous when it comes to asking the tough questions, but it's a different story when it comes to self-promotion.

In fact, journalists are usually the last ones to toot their own horns when it comes to their successes. And when they speak to my students at San Francisco State University or UC Berkeley, professional journalists are even more humble about the work that has propelled their careers at some of the biggest news outlets in the country.

While humility should be viewed as a noble trait, it can be deadly to anyone trying to promote themselves and their work within digital and social media. With so many people sharing their insight on everything from food to travel to politics, journalists and newsrooms must speak up. But posting a link and telling random folks on Facebook, for example, is not the way to convince others to read all about it.

To have the most success in reaching your target audience and getting them to read, listen to, or view your work, you'll need to first identify your target audience.

How to Identify Your Target Audience

Decide which demographic you want to target. To determine the demographics, answer the following questions:

- How expensive is the subscription to your news outlet? Or is it free? Do you have a **paywall** (meaning that your audience can read a certain number of stories before they have to pay)?
- Are your stories mainly about men or women? How old are the subjects in your stories? Who would be most interested in those stories?
- Do you write about a particular neighborhood? Or do you provide statewide, national or international coverage?

- Do your stories focus on certain themes, such as social justice, technology, or adventure travel? Do your stories share common values?
- What do you want your target audience to do? Read your stories and watch your videos to gain knowledge? Be entertained? (Think back to the audience needs under the Uses and Gratification Theory.)

Once you have answered these questions, you should have a basic understanding of your target audience.

Finding the Right Social Networks

While the Pew Research Center reported in 2018 that that Facebook and YouTube "dominate this landscape," it found that the most popular networks among people 18 to 24 in age were Instagram and Snapchat.[1]

Identify the Behavior of Your Target Audience

Another key factor in choosing the right networks is to understand how users behave on each network. Every network has a different look and feel. It also attracts a different set of users or audience members. Keep in mind of those differences when posting to each platform.

Communicate With Your Target Audience

In the old days, paid advertising was the best – albeit costly – way for newsrooms to promote their work. While it remains vital to a company's social and digital media strategy, many smaller newsrooms, start-ups, and journalists may not be able to afford the cost of paying for ads on social networks, search engines, and websites.

In addition, paid advertising on social media may not be the most effective way to reach your target audience.

"Social media is adopting its own form of SEO in a way that promotes a positive user experience," according to Mention, a company that offers web and social media monitoring. "The way this algorithm works is by putting your posts in a pool as small as one percent of your followers. If those people engage with the content, then it gets introduced into a larger pool. Slowly but surely, more and more people see it, but only if it's engaging."[2]

In an effort to spark more "meaningful interactions," Facebook announced in 2018 that users would see less public content. "Because space in News Feed is limited, showing more posts from friends and family and updates that spark conversation means we'll show less public content, including videos and other posts from publishers or businesses," Zuckerberg said in a statement.[3]

To do this, he explained, Facebook "will predict which posts you might want to interact with your friends about, and show these posts higher in feed. These are posts that inspire back-and-forth discussion in the comments and posts that you might want to share and react to – whether that's a post from a friend seeking advice, a friend asking for recommendations for a trip, or a news article or video prompting lots of discussion."[4]

Organic Reach

That is why it's important to understand how to increase the **organic reach** of your content. Organic reach on social media is simply defined as how well your posts perform without any money behind them. To boost your organic reach, you'll want to learn how to promote your work in a way that resonates with your target audience so THEY can help **amplify** your message.

"Amplification happens when your content is shared, either through organic or paid engagement, within social marketing channels thereby increasing your word-of-mouth exposure," according to the content marketing team at gShift. "Amplification works by getting your message promoted (amplified) through employees, customers, industry partners, fans and influencers."[5]

An influencer in the world of social media is simply defined as someone who has influence over his or her followers and can get them to act on certain issues. While there is no set number, an influencer usually has at least 2,000 followers on a given platform.

"The right influencer is someone who can reach your target audience, build trust, and drive engagement," according to Hootsuite. "They will create original, engaging content that is in line with their own brand (rather than following a template advertising style provided by a brand)."[6]

Of course, influencers are only one group of people you should be trying to reach. Quality followers, friends, and connections are equally important. Below you'll find a good tip sheet on how to create a social media strategy to boost your organic reach.

Ten Ways to Increase Your Organic Reach on Social Media

1 **Build quality followers**

While CNN's Anderson Cooper has nearly ten million followers on Twitter, quantity is far less important than the *quality*. That's because if followers never share, retweet or like your content, you will have very few people to amplify your story, which means very few people will see it. A tweet has an average shelf life of 18 minutes![7] Posts on other platforms last a bit longer. For example, a post on Facebook can last about five hours before it fades, Instagram about 21 hours and YouTube for 20 days or more.

2 **Use the 80–20 rule when sharing content**

If you were sitting with a friend having coffee, would you tell them all about the great things you're doing? Or, would you also want to know what they are up to? How about making them laugh? Social media should be treated the same way.

Eighty percent of your content should be useful and helpful to your followers and potential followers, while only 20 percent should be about you or your latest story. This is tough for most journalists, because some only want to share when they have a new story to promote. But remember this: social media is meant to be social. If you're having a one-way conversation with people who are connected to you, they will soon turn you off or stop following you.

3   **Join conversations by using hashtags and mentioning others**

"Just like you use keywords to attract visitors to your website, hashtags are crucial if you want to increase your exposure on social media," says Monique Holtman of UK Domain. "Twitter and Instagram are where hashtags are most commonly used so you should always try to use them when posting on these channels. Hashtags help to bring more people to your pages because anyone searching for the word you've used will see your post. It is however important to stay on topic. You shouldn't be commenting or posting on everything that's trending – it must be relevant to your business."[8]

To discover trending hashtags, you can go on any social network and slowly start to type keywords in the search box, or you can use tools and apps like Hashtagify.

Hashtagify will allow you to type in a keyword to find out what's trending. It will even help you find influencers, which was described earlier as people who can help amplify your message to their followers.

4   **Use attention-catching visuals**

Fact: "The average person gets distracted in **eight seconds**, though a mere 2.8 seconds is enough to distract some people."[9] This list offers even more facts you should know about visuals for social and digital media.

5   **Post at the right times, but don't over post!**

Some research shows that you should post during slow hours."[10]

Though opinions on when to post can differ quite a bit, these are generally thought to be the best times to post:

- Facebook –between 1 p.m. and 4 p.m.
- Twitter –during the lunch hour of 12 p.m. to 1 p.m.
- LinkedIn –between 10 a.m. and 11 a.m.And remember, don't over post! Buffer, a social media management tool, also suggests how often to post.[11]

6   **How often to post to social media**

- Facebook – once per day is optimal, with a maximum of two posts per day. Hubspot found that pages under 10,000 fans experienced a 50 percent drop in engagement *per post* if they posted more than once per day."

- Twitter – this number can vary, depending on who you talk to, but many agree that 3 to 30 times a day is optimal.
- LinkedIn – no more than once a day.
- Pinterest – three Pins per day, with a maximum of 30 Pins per day.
- Instagram – at least once per day, and no more than three times per day.
- YouTube – the number varys, but most agree that you have to be consistent on YouTube.[12]

7 **Cross-promote**

Different people will be on different platforms at different times. So, the key here is to cross-promote your content, which essentially means toot your horn on Twitter when you share something on LinkedIn and vice versa. Some of these networks make it easy for you to do this with just a click of a button.

8 **Engage. Engage. Engage.**

"While we normally discuss promotion on social media as a function of promoted posts, engagement and redistribution are ways that journalists promote their content organically on social platforms," wrote the authors of the Cision 2017 Global Social Journalism Study.[13] The study found that 66 percent of journalists reported engaging with readers at least daily.

Kara Swisher of the technology news site Recode is "an example of a very high-frequency engager, responding to unsolicited comments as well as comments on her published articles," according to Cision.[14]

UK Domain adds that if you "properly engage with people and reply to their comments, you're going to build a great reputation that will spread. People will look for your posts because they'll be genuinely interested in what you're doing. Forging that kind of bond is important for all aspects of your business, but it can create a viral effect for your organic reach."[15]

9 **Measure your success and change to improve engagement**

The Online Advertising Guide advice is to ensure that you measure the engagement rate of your posts. The engagement rate is typically defined as the percentage of people who saw a piece of content or ad and engaged with it. "For example if one person interacted one time with an ad after it has had 100 ad impressions, that will give you an ER of 1 percent."[16]

Conclusion

Focus on quality over quantity when it comes to everything from followers to actual content. "The secret to organic social media reach is the same as the secret to ranking well on search engines," according to the writers at Mention. "It's all about optimization, user experience, and high-quality content."[17]

Discussion Questions

1   Why do you think quality is more important than quantity?
2   What are some of the easiest ways to promote your content?
3   Look at the social accounts of *National Geographic*. What does this media company do to stand out? Is that something that can be replicated? How so?

Exercises

1   Go to the Twitter accounts of at least three well-known journalists. Note how many followers each has. Note how many people liked and commented on their two most recent tweets.
2   Using the formula to measure engagement, did those tweets do well? Explain why or why not.

Notes

1 Aaron Smith and Monica Anderson, "Social Media Use in 2018: A majority of Americans use Facebook and YouTube, but young adults are especially heavy users of Snapchat and Instagram," *Pew Research Center*, March 1, 2018, https://www.pewinternet.org/2018/03/01/social-media-use-in-2018/, accessed March 21, 2019.
2 Mention, https://mention.com/en/
3 Facebook Newsroom, "Bringing People Closer Together," January 11, 2018, https://newsroom.fb.com/news/2018/01/news-feed-fyi-bringing-people-closer-together/, accessed March 21, 2019.
4 Ibid.
5 gShift.com, "What is social amplification?" https://www.gshiftlabs.com/social-media-blog/social-amplification-part-1-of-3-what-is-social-amplification/, accessed September 8, 2018.
6 Hootsuite, https://blog.hootsuite.com/influencer-marketing/.
7 Breanne Sagan, "How long does content last and how frequently should you post on social media," Sprockets Website, June 28, 2018, https://www.sprocketwebsites.com/Blog/how-long-does-content-last-and-how-frequently-should-you-post-on-social-media, accessed July 26, 2018.
8 Monique Holtman, "How to grow your social media followers to strengthen your brand," UK Domain, October 31, 2017, https://www.theukdomain.uk/grow-social-media-followers-strengthen-brand/, accessed August 13, 2018.
9 https://webdam.com/blog/brand-marketing-infographic
10 Mention, https://mention.com/blog/organic-social-media-reach/
11 https://www.oberlo.com/blog/best-time-post-social-media.

12 Louise Myers, "How Often To Post On Social Media: 2019 Success Guide", March 25, 2019, https://louisem.com/144557/often-post-social-media.

13 Cision 2017 Global Social Journalism Study, https://www.cision.com/us/2017/09/how-successful-journalists-use-social-media/.

14 Annemaria Nicholson, "How Successful Journalists Use Social Media," September 20, 2017, Cision 2017 Global Social Journalism Study, https://www.cision.com/us/2017/09/how-successful-journalists-use-social-media/, accessed March 28, 2019.

15 Monique Holtman, "How to grow your social media followers to strengthen your brand," UK Domain, October 31, 2017, https://www.theukdomain.uk/grow-social-media-followers-strengthen-brand/, accessed August 13, 2018.

16 The Online Advertising Guide, https://theonlineadvertisingguide.com/glossary/engagement-rate/, accessed November 8, 2018.

17 Mention, https://mention.com/blog/organic-social-media-reach/

11 Importance of Measuring Your Success

Figure 11.1 Return on Investment. Credit: Alexmillos. Getty Images.

In today's fast-changing media landscape, it's critical for news organizations to incorporate the use of analytics into their newsroom strategies. That's because analytics – the "systematic analysis of quantitative data on various aspects of audience behavior" – can help build audience, increase engagement, and improve newsroom workflows.[1]

A 2016 Reuters Institute report "Editorial Analytics: How News Media Are Developing and Using Audience Data and Metrics," states that "News organizations today are competing for attention in an ever-more competitive and constantly changing media environment . . . No one can take their audience for granted. The battle for attention is a central challenge for journalism because its public role is premised on connecting with an audience – as is the business model of private news media and the legitimacy of public service media."[2]

The authors of the report, Federica Cherubini and Rasmus Kleis Nielsen, discovered that *The Guardian*, the *Financial Times*, and the BBC were some of the biggest news organizations in Europe and the United States following the lead of BuzzFeed, Gawker, and other smaller, digital-only sites in using analytics to determine consumer behavior and build a larger audience.

"We see how old metrics like pageviews and unique browsers are increasingly accompanied by new measures of social interactions, engaged time, and loyalty," they wrote, adding that new social media monitoring tools such as Chartbeat, Parse.ly, and NewsWhip supplement Google Analytics, Facebook Insights, and other more traditional tools.

Cherubini and Nielsen added, however, that newsrooms had the most success when they devised a system of analytics to measure their own unique goals. *The Wall Street Journal*, for example, had a special team that focused on increasing subscription and engagement. In fact, the *The Wall Street Journal* was looking for brand ambassadors to "promote activations through traditional and alternative tactics" with a strong understanding of how to leverage social media. Its magazine was also seeking to hire a digital editor to work closely with the digital director to launch and scale a "digital-first iteration of the magazine."[3]

Start by Creating a Social Media Marketing Strategy

Before setting up your own system of measuring success, you'll need to establish your objectives and goals. Do you want more subscribers? To increase digital advertising? To build brand awareness? To find new talent? Each goal should be **SMART**, which means it is:

- Specific
- Measurable
- Attainable
- Relevant
- Time-bound

SMART goals allow you to measure your social media return on investment (ROI), defined as the "sum of all social media actions that create value."[4]

Once you have established your goals, you should create a **social media marketing** (SMM) strategy to target certain social networks and applications to "spread brand awareness or promote particular products."[5]

Techopedia says your SMM strategy should basically do three things:

1   Establish a social media presence on major platforms.
2   Create shareable content and advertorials.
3   Cultivate customer feedback throughout the campaign through surveys and contests.

A good example of how to apply SMART goals to a project follows.

SMART Goal

In order to establish myself as an expert, I will write a 150-page book on social media by writing one chapter per month (or three to five pages per week). The book will be completed in 10 months, and then I will search for a publisher or explore self-publishing.

- Specific: I will write a book about social media that is a minimum of 150 pages.
- Measurable: I will write one chapter per month, or three to five pages per week.
- Attainable: I will work on the manuscript first, and once that is completed, I will begin to search for a publisher or explore self-publishing.
- Relevant: Writing a book on social media will help me establish myself as an expert.
- Time-Based: My manuscript will be completed and ready to be published in 10 months.

Alyssa Gregory, founder of the Small Business Bonfire, a community for entrepreneurs; and Small Business Expert for The Balance.

Pay to Play

In a perfect world, everything would be free, including how we reach our target audience on social media. But the ability of businesses to reach their potential clients and customers organically has dropped precipitously low on Facebook and other social networks. As early as 2012, Facebook announced that "Pages organically reach about 16 percent of their fans on average." That number has only gone down in recent years. Facebook's advice has and continues to be this: "To make sure your fans see your stories, sponsor your posts to increase the reach of your content."[6]

So, if you really want to promote your news site and work to others, you'll need to consider paying for some of your advertising. Even if you have a small budget, advertising on social media can be relatively cheap. That's because most networks give you the option of sponsoring just one post at a time.

Most social networks offer a step-by-step guide to users interested in sponsoring or promoting a particular post or tweet, and they will also help you launch campaigns.

The majority of networks also provide you detailed analytics to show you how many people you reached with your post or tweet. The key thing to remember is that, just because you pay to promote a post, it won't do well unless you remember some of the basic concepts of what makes good content on social media, which were discussed earlier in this book.

Understanding the Importance of Google

SEO, briefly stated, is the "process website owners use to help search engines find, index, and rank their web pages, hopefully above competitors' websites. While there are several search engines you can rank on, including Bing and Yahoo, the majority of Internet search (80 percent) is done through Google."[7]

Google Ads, which was previously Google AdWords, is an online advertising system developed by Google in which advertisers "pay to display brief advertisements, service offerings, product listings, and video content within the *Google* ad network to web users."[8]

The system is based partly on cookies and partly on keywords determined by advertisers. Google uses these characteristics to place advertising copy on pages where they think it might be relevant. Advertisers pay when users divert their browsing to click on the advertising copy. Partner websites receive a portion of the generated income. See https://ads.google.com/home/how-it-works/.

Google Analytics provides an easy way to compare the performance of each page to the rest of the content on your site. If you have a paid media budget, you can promote the most popular ones as a piece of native advertising, to spread your reach to other like-minded people too.

Measuring Traffic to Your Website

If your objective is to increase traffic to your site, focus on increasing your clicks and **clickthrough rate** (CTR), defined as the percentage of people visiting a web page who access a hypertext link to a particular advertisement. To do this, you'll want to use keywords that are highly relevant and very compelling to your audience.

Conclusion

Analytics are critical to understand what works with an increasingly mobile audience.

"Many journalists also want analytics, as an earlier period of scepticism seems to have given way to interest in how data and metrics can help newsrooms reach their target audiences and do better journalism," wrote Cherubini and Nielsen, and that is encouraging, because analytics and data metrics will continue to evolve, and if journalists are not part of that process, the tools and techniques developed will continue to reflect and empower commercial and technological priorities more than editorial priorities."[9]

There are some pitfalls, however, to measuring success by the number of clicks one receives.

"A reckless use of audience metrics can however lead to 'culture of the click' in newsrooms," Laura Vermeire wrote in her essay on newsroom analytics. "The audience's desires become a central element in editorial decision-making as news websites are giving in to a survival instinct and therefore adopt a market-oriented policy."[10]

Discussion Questions

1   How might the use of analytics hurt the goals of a newsroom seeking to cover stories about poverty or race?
2   Is the number of clicks the most important thing in journalism? Why or why not?
3   Should newsrooms receive public funding to sustain their efforts to produce quality journalism? Why or why not?

Exercises

1   In groups, create a Business page on a social network of your choice. Research how much it will cost to promote a post or tweet and try to find out the least amount of money one can spend to promote a post or tweet and what the reach will be. Then explain in a short essay whether it's worth promoting the post or tweet for that amount of money.
2   Research some of the top brands on Facebook. Study how many people like, share, or comment on their most recent posts. Explain in a short essay how many of those posts were sponsored.
3   Check out your news feed on Instagram for three days. How many of those posts are sponsored by brands? What type of

content are you seeing. Why do you think that content is showing up in your news feed? Please explain in a short essay.

4   Review the steps on how to create a Google Ads campaign.
Decide as a group or individual what produce or content you
would promote with the Google Ads campaign and explain in
three-page report.

Notes

1   Federica Cherubini and Rasmus Kleis Nielsen, "News media are developing and
using audience data and metrics," Reuters Institute, February 23, 2016, http://
www.digitalnewsreport.org/publications/2016/editorial-analytics-2016/,
accessed August 14, 2018.

2   Ibid.

3   Google Jobs, WSJ listings on September 10, 2018, https://www.google.com/sear
ch?q=Wall+Street+Journal&ibp=htl;jobs&rciv=jb&hl=en&gl=US#fpstate=tld
etail&htidocid=6nEOPWmB2H_EiWcYAAAAAA%3D%3D&htivrt=jobs

4   Hootsuite, https://blog.hootsuite.com/measure-social-media-roi-business/#
whatis

5   Techopedia, https://www.techopedia.com/definition/5396/social-media-mark
eting-smm

6   Facebook Business, https://www.facebook.com/marketing/posts/pages-organically-
reach-about-16-of-their-fans-on-average-to-make-sure-your-fans/
10150839503836337/

7   Randy Duermyer, "Search Engine Optimization Tutorial," Balance Small
Business, April 8, 2018, https://www.thebalancesmb.com/search-engine-opti
mization-tutorial-1794804, accessed August 3, 2018.

8   Google Ads, https://ads.google.com/home/how-it-works/

9   Federica Cherubini and Rasmus Kleis Nielsen, "News media are developing and
using audience data and metrics," Reuters Institute, February 23, 2016, http://
www.digitalnewsreport.org/publications/2016/editorial-analytics-2016/,
accessed March 19, 2019.

10   Laura Vermeire, "A culture of clicks: How audience metrics can help online
news editors, publishers and journalists become more successful," *Medium,* Nov.
12, 2017. https://medium.com/journalism-trends-technologies/a-culture-of-
clicks-58719857b934, accessed March 20, 2019.

12 Social Media for Public Relations

Social media has not only impacted everything we know about journalism, but it has also impacted everything we know about **public relations** (PR), defined as the ability to control the "spread of information between an organization or an individual and the public."[1]

The rise of social media has forced PR firms to understand how to leverage social media to persuade people to care about their issues or think favorably about their candidates, clients, and companies.

Nowadays, clients, customers, and others can wield a lot of power over a politician, company, or celebrity because tweets and public social media posts have the potential to go viral. This has prompted many companies and PR firms to embrace social media as an integral part of their communications strategy, including setting up public social accounts with staff dedicated to monitoring and responding to those concerns in real-time, 24–7.

While social media has "touched just about every industry under the sun in some capacity, it has had a huge—and arguably more pointed—impact on the public relations industry," Jessica Lawlor wrote in Ragan's PR Daily. "From changing the way people consume their news to contributing to the rise of the citizen journalist, social media has forced PR pros and reporters to adapt or perish."[2]

There are many similarities between PR and journalism: both seek to create information and share it with a mass audience, for example. One big difference is that journalists seek to tell the good, bad, and ugly about the world around them, and PR professionals usually want to offer the positive light on the people or companies they represent. Novelist George Orwell said it best: "Journalism is printing what someone else does not want printed; everything else is public relations."[3]

Within many universities, the study of PR is housed within their journalism schools, departments, and programs.

Beyond college, you'll soon discover that many former newspaper or TV news reporters are now working PR professionals, representing public agencies, politicians, Fortune 500 companies, and many others. These journalists may not have been trained in PR, but they do know how to research, write well, and communicate effectively.

Another thing that professional journalists bring to PR is that they know what it takes to make the front page or top of the news hour. They understand the values of news, the importance of meeting deadlines, and many have great connections to the newsrooms that PR firms are trying to reach.

As we learned earlier in the book, journalists must also understand how to leverage social media for their jobs as storytellers, fact checkers, messengers of truth, and so on – as do PR professionals.

Theoretical Framework for Understanding PR

Author and researcher James E. Grunig, among the most well-known PR scholars of our time, says there are four models of public relations:

- The **Press Agentry Publicity Model** follows "one-way communication where the flow of information is only from the sender to the receiver. The sender is not much concerned about the second party's feedback, reviews and so on. In Press Agentry publicity model, public relations experts enhance the reputation of the organization among the target audiences, stakeholders, employees, partners, investors and all others associated with it through manipulation."
- The **Public Information Model** "revolves around one-way communication where information primarily flows from sender (organization and public relations experts) to the receiver (target audience, employees, stakeholders, employees, investors and so on)." This model also "emphasizes on maintaining and enhancing the image of an organization simply by circulating relevant and meaningful information among the target audience/public. Public relations experts depend on press release, news release, video release or any other recorded communication often directed at the media to circulate information about their brand among the public."

    NOTE: A **press release** is defined by Merriam-Webster as an "official statement that gives information to newspapers, magazines, television news programs, and radio stations, and a **press conference is** defined as "an interview or announcement given by a public figure to the press by appointment."
- The **Two-Way Asymmetrical Model** "revolves around two-way communication between both the parties but the communication is somewhat not balanced. In this type of model, public relations experts position their organization and brand on the whole in the minds of their target audiences through manipulation and force the public to behave the same way they would want them to do."
- The **Two-Way Symmetrical Model** attempts to create a mutually beneficial situation. This model "revolves around two-way communication where PR professionals seek to "position their brand among end-users. Free flow of information takes place between the organization

and its stakeholders, employees, investors and vice-a-versa. Conflicts and misunderstandings are resolved through mutual discussions and communication."[4]

In today's world, the "ideal way of enhancing an organization's reputation among the target audience" is to follow the two-way symmetrical model, according to Grunig. He and many other noted scholars believe that this is the most "ethical model, one that professionals should aspire to use in their everyday tactics and strategies."[5]

In the two-way symmetrical model, the "public relations practitioner should serve as a liaison between the organization and key publics, rather than as a persuader," wrote communications lecturer Jasmine Roberts of Ohio State University in her book, Writing for Communication Industries. "Here, practitioners are negotiators and use communication to ensure that all involved parties benefit, not just the organization that employs them. The term 'symmetrical' is used because the model attempts to create a mutually beneficial situation."[6]

PR professionals should still send out press releases and contact newsrooms to get the coverage they want, but they must also learn how to leverage social and digital media to engage with an increasingly fragmented audience – and journalists.

While social media can be a great place to research reporters and make connections, it's not a good idea to tweet or direct message your pitch directly to a reporter unless their bio explicitly indicates to do so," Lawlor says.[7] For pitching stories, following the two main formats, email and phone."

To find journalists who might cover your products, clients, and services, use a search engine to conduct some research. Find out the kinds of stories a particular journalist produces and where the journalist has worked BEFORE you reach out. Check out public profiles on social networks, and see if journalists are open to connecting or hearing from you. Some will say right on their profiles or within their summaries that they're happy to hear about story ideas.

Tip: Avoid trying to friend or connect with people you don't know. Journalists are not quick to trust strangers, and very few will accept an invite from people they cover. Do, however, try to follow their public profiles and engage with them through likes, retweets, and comments.

Going Beyond Traditional Journalists

Nowadays, PR professionals can go beyond the usual suspects in the traditional news media to spread their messaging.

"Roughly 6,000 tweets are shared per second on Twitter. That's just one of many social networks," Lawlor of Ragan's PR Daily wrote. "While that makes social media a highly effective tool for communicating breaking news coverage, it also means the lifespan of a news story is much shorter than it used to be. This means that journalists are constantly searching for the next big thing and PR pros must keep up."[8]

Six Things to Do When Reaching Out to Journalists and Other Influencers

1   Don't try to friend or connect with a journalist or influencer – unless you know them personally.
2   Do follow their public profiles, and like, retweet, or comment on their posts.
3   Spend some time interacting with journalists and influencers before sending them a direct message or post asking them to cover your story. If it's urgent, however, let journalists know that you have a good story and offer it as an exclusive.
4   Depending on the kind of PR you do, you may want to send your product directly to journalists and influencers so they can try it out, or invite them for a special tour or event. Many entertainers send journalists free tickets to the opening of a new concert or show, and some will invite journalists to a movie before it opens to the public.
5   Be sure that your client is available to chat with the news media, either in person or by phone. You may want to use tools such as Facebook Live or Skype to set up virtual meetings, too.
6   Most important, make sure you're available to answer the journalist's call when they need you. For influencers, this may be a bit different because they may not face the same deadlines that most people working for a network or newspaper have.

Monitoring Reputation in Today's World

A big part of what PR professionals do is to manage the reputation of their clients. This used to be as simple as perusing the big papers and watching the news. Nowadays, you'll have to figure out how to stay on top of the world wide web and beyond. Luckily, there are plenty of tools, some free and others quite pricey, that can help you do this.

Perhaps the cheapest and easiest thing to do is set up a Google alert that can notify you any time your client is in the news. You'll want to use key terms that deal with your brand, names of people who work for the brand, and products associated with your brand. You might even want to stay on top of the competition by setting up alerts for them. Here are just a few tools that can help:

Buzzsumo is a paid product that allows you see the most shared content during selected time periods on Facebook, LinkedIn, Twitter, and Pinterest.

CoSchedule has a paid version that helps with everything from monitoring trending topics to promoting content.

TweetDeck will let you set up Twitter alerts to stay on top of what people are saying about your brand.

Conclusion

There are many more tools, which are constantly changing, but be sure to figure out a system that helps you to manage your client's reputation online and off.

Discussion Questions

1   What similarities are there between PR and journalism?
2   What are the differences?
3   Should PR professionals still send out press releases, or simply rely on the social and digital ecosystem to get their messages out? Why or why not?
4   Do you think social media helps or hurts PR people as they try to get the word out about their clients, customers, and products?

Exercises

1   In teams, come up with a PR strategy to promote a story about social justice on campus that includes traditional and newer forms of promotion. Present your strategy as a slideshow in class.
2   Imagine you are trying to reach a reporter for an event that is happening tomorrow. You email that person, but she or he has not gotten back to you. How might you reach this reporter under deadline pressure? Please explain in a short essay.

Notes

1 James E. Grunig and Todd Hunt. "Managing Public Relations," New York, Holt, Rinehart and Winston, 1984.
2 Jessica Lawlor, "5 ways social media has reshaped the PR industry," Ragan's PR Daily, November 7, 2018, https://www.prdaily.com/5-ways-social-media-has-reshaped-the-pr-industry/, accessed March 28, 2019.
3 Goodreads.com, https://www.goodreads.com/quotes/77244-journalism-is-printing-what-someone-else-does-not-want-printed
4 Grunig, James E., Grunig, Larissa A., Sriramesh, K., Huang, Yi-Hui, Lyra, Anastasia, *Journal of Public Relations Research*, July 1, 1995, Vol.7(3), pp. 163–186.
5 Jasmine Roberts, "Writing for strategic communication industries", Ohio State University, http://solr.bccampus.ca:8001/bcc/file/cb278124-0378-4dc4-87f3-a0bb635a24c9/1/Writing-for-Strategic-Communication-Industries-1474040746.pdf
6 Ibid.
7 Jessica Lawlor, "5 ways social media has reshaped the PR industry," Ragan's PR Daily, November 7, 2018, https://www.prdaily.com/5-ways-social-media-has-reshaped-the-pr-industry/, accessed March 28, 2019.
8 Ibid.

Glossary

actual malice A defendant's publication of a statement either knowing it was false or carelessly, without checking whether it was true or false.

Agenda-Setting Theory Theory that states that in editors, newsroom staff, and broadcasters play an important part in shaping political reality.

amplification When content is shared, either through organic or paid engagement, within social marketing channels thereby increasing your word-of-mouth exposure.

anecdotal lead Person or issue described in the lead or top of the story who exemplifies a problem that affects many more people.

Audience Engagement Editor Editor who oversees an audience strategy.

character attributes Attributes including persona or character, tone, language, and purpose.

citizen journalism Journalism conducted by people who are not professional journalists but disseminate information around the world. Citizen journalism has expanded worldwide with people in disaster zones providing live or on-the-scene information that no one else has.

Content Coach Team leader who creates social media strategy to build and engage an audience.

content curation the act of discovering, gathering, and presenting digital content that surrounds specific subject matter.

content management system (CMS) A software application or set of related programs that are used to create and manage digital content.

customer journey The complete sum of experiences that customers go through when interacting with your company and brand.

Digital First A business practice in which the internet drives all decisions regarding how news is covered, in what form, by whom, and when.

echo chamber A "situation where certain ideas, beliefs or data points are reinforced through repetition of a closed system that does not allow for the free movement of alternative or competing ideas or concepts. In an echo chamber, there is the implication that certain ideas or outcomes win out because of an inherent unfairness in how input is gathered."

Four Theories of Press model A theoretical framework that defines four major theories behind the functioning of the world's presses—(1) the **Authoritarian Theory**, which developed in the late Renaissance and was based on the idea that truth is the product of a few wise men; (2) the **Libertarian Theory**, which arose from the works of Milton, Locke, Mill, and Jefferson and avowed that the search for truth is one of man's natural rights; (3) the **Social Responsibility Theory** of the modern day, equal radio and television time for political candidates, the obligations of the newspaper in a one-paper town, and so on; (4) the **Soviet Communist Theory**, an expanded and more positive version of the old Authoritarian Theory.

Fourth Estate A term used to refer to the press or news media. In medieval Europe, the people who participated in the political life of a country were generally divided into three classes or estates. In England they were the three groups with representation in Parliament, namely, the nobility, the clergy, and the common people. Some other group, like the mob or the public press, that had an unofficial but often great influence on public affairs, was called the fourth estate. In the 19th century, fourth estate came to refer exclusively to the press, and now it's applied to all branches of the news media.

gatekeeper Person or entity who decides what information should move to group or individual and what information should not.

Gatekeeping Theory Theory under which owners, publishers, and editors of newspapers were considered the gatekeepers of news and information for the general public.

Hutchins Commission Commission formed by a small group of powerful journalist and educators after World War II in response to public outcry over elitism, sensationalism, and media conglomeration. The commission came up with five recommendations to address the public's concerns: (1) truthful, comprehensive, and intelligent account of the day's events; (2) a forum for the exchange of comment and criticism; (3) the projection of a representative picture of the constituent groups in the society; (4) the presentation and clarification of the goals and values of the society; (5) full access to the day's intelligence.

influencer Someone who has influence over his or her followers and can get them to act on certain issues. While there is no set number, an influencer usually has at least 2,000 followers on a given platform.

Information Age The modern age regarded as a time in which information has become a commodity that is quickly and widely disseminated and easily available, especially through the use of computer technology.

journalism crowdsourcing The act of specifically inviting a group of people to participate in a reporting task—such as newsgathering, data collection, or analysis—through a targeted, open call for input; personal experiences; documents; or other contributions.

libel   False and defamatory attack in written form on a person's reputation or character.

Libertarian Theory   Theory of the press, which states that interference from kings or governors should be restrained.

Maslow's Hierarchy of Needs   A motivational theory in psychology comprising a five-tier model of human needs, often depicted as hierarchical levels within a pyramid. Needs lower down in the hierarchy must be satisfied before individuals can attend to needs higher up. From the bottom of the hierarchy upwards, the needs are: physiological, safety, love and belonging, esteem, and self-actualization.

Multimedia Journalist (MMJ)/**Multiskilled Journalists** (MSJ) (also known as **All Media Journalist, Digital Reporter,** and **Digital Storyteller**)   Journalist who gathers information, writes stories, makes broadcasts, and uses social media to keep the public informed about current affairs and events that are happening in the world, often combining text, images, sound, videos, and graphics to tell an interesting story.

objectivity norm   A standard followed by journalists seeking to be impartial, detached, balanced, and accurate in their reporting of news.

organic reach   How well your posts perform on social media without any money behind them.

paywall   An arrangement whereby access to a website is restricted to users who have paid to subscribe to the site.

personal brand   A term coined by motivational speaker and author Tom Peters in 1997 to signify who you are, what you stand for, and how others perceive you. The personal brand is made up of your bio, your profile, your photos, your activities, your causes, your stories, and even your tweets and social posts.

personal brand statement   An "elevator pitch" or narrative that succinctly describes one's skills, interests, and other attributes.

podcast   A digital audio file made available on the Internet for downloading to a computer or mobile device, typically available as a series, new installments of which can be received by subscribers automatically.

press releases   Announcements sent to the news media.

public figures   People whose achievements or notoriety places them in the public eye, or people who seek attention by voluntarily thrusting themselves into a public controversy.

public officials   Elected officials and candidates. Appointed officials may or may not be public officials. Criteria: Do they have the authority to set policy in the government and are they under public scrutiny to have easy access to the media?

scoop   A piece of important or exciting news that is revealed by before other news outlets know about it.

search engine optimization (SEO)   A methodology of strategies, techniques, and tactics used to increase the amount of visitors to a website by obtaining a high-ranking placement in the search results page of a search engine,

slander   False and defamatory attack in oral form.

Social Media Reporter   Reporter who supplements traditional news reporting by adding informative content in media conduits such as blogs, microblogs (such as Twitter), websites, web pages, and other platforms.

Social Media Video Producer   Producer who drives a social and digital video strategy.

Social Velocity Reporter   Reporter expected to make split-second decisions and understand the tools, trends, platforms, and processes behind the most modern strategies for telling stories via social media.

Social Media Editor   Professional who manages and grows a news outlet or organization's social footprint across the web.

verified   Confirmed to be authentic by a social network. Verification is often indicated by a blue check.

verticals   Types of publication whereby the content is primarily focused on one particular type of business or industry.

viral   Material, such as an article, an image or a video that spreads rapidly online through website links and social sharing.

vlog   A blog in which the postings are primarily in video form.

Index

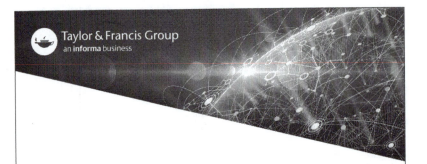

Taylor & Francis eBooks

www.taylorfrancis.com

A single destination for eBooks from Taylor & Francis
with increased functionality and an improved user
experience to meet the needs of our customers.

90,000+ eBooks of award-winning academic content in
Humanities, Social Science, Science, Technology, Engineering,
and Medical written by a global network of editors and authors.

TAYLOR & FRANCIS EBOOKS OFFERS:

A streamlined
experience for
our library
customers

A single point
of discovery
for all of our
eBook content

Improved
search and
discovery of
content at both
book and
chapter level

REQUEST A FREE TRIAL
support@taylorfrancis.com